VANISHED

HOUSTON
LANDMARKS

VANISHED
HOUSTON
LANDMARKS

MARK LARDAS

THE
History
PRESS

Published by The History Press
Charleston, SC
www.historypress.com

Copyright © 2020 by Mark Lardas

First published 2020

Manufactured in the United States

ISBN 9781467142816

Library of Congress Control Number: 2019951872

Notice: The information in this book is true and complete to the best of our knowledge. It is offered without guarantee on the part of the author or The History Press. The author and The History Press disclaim all liability in connection with the use of this book.

To my new daughter-in-law, Khai (Vicky) Hoan Nguyen Lardas.
Welcome to the United States and Houston.

CONTENTS

CONTENTS

ACKNOWLEDGEMENTS

N o book is the product of a single author. Many folks helped me as I wrote and assembled this book. Those who I especially would like to note include:

The Helen Hall Library in League City went above and beyond in providing materials from its Local History Collection and securing other material through interlibrary loan. This local public library is a great starting point for any researcher.

The University of Houston provided support in acquiring digital images. I have deep gratitude for Bethany Scott, Emily Vinson and Don Geraciat at the University of Houston. They went above and beyond the call of duty to help me get images from the university's digital archives.

A similar thanks goes out to Matt Richardson, photography archive supervisor; the Houston Metropolitan Research Center at the Houston Public Library; and Sandra Cherry at the Lunar and Planetary Institute.

I would also like to acknowledge the following individuals and organizations that provided photos for this book: Marianne Avioliotis, Marianne Dyson, Bill Hensel (Port of Houston Authority), Paul Hester, the Houston Maritime Museum, William Lardas, John Lardas, Brian Reading and John H. Smith.

I would also like to thank Ben Gibson and Ashley Hill, my editors at The History Press, for their assistance.

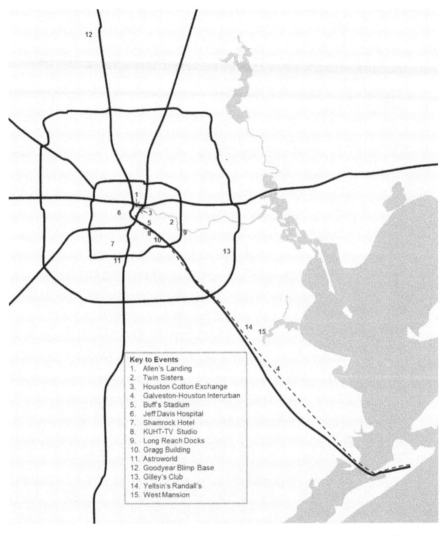

Key to Events
1. Allen's Landing
2. Twin Sisters
3. Houston Cotton Exchange
4. Galveston-Houston Interurban
5. Buff's Stadium
6. Jeff Davis Hospital
7. Shamrock Hotel
8. KUHT-TV Studio
9. Long Reach Docks
10. Gragg Building
11. Astroworld
12. Goodyear Blimp Base
13. Gilley's Club
14. Yeltsin's Randall's
15. West Mansion

The locations of the fifteen items presented in this book. They range from Spring, Texas, (Goodyear Blimp Bases) to Galveston, Texas (Galveston–Houston Electric Railroad). *Drawing by author.*

INTRODUCTION

Houston is often accused of being a city without a history—or at least a city that has forgotten its history. The first accusation is nonsense; Houston has a history—over 180 years of history. While much of Houston's history is local, some of it has literally changed the world. As to the accusation that Houston has forgotten its history, that has more foundation. Houstonians have traditionally been unsentimental about their historic landmarks; if something has outlived its usefulness, Houstonians typically yank it out and replace it with something more remunerative. It is a Houston tradition, so who are traditionalists to cry foul on a tradition? For that matter, if Houstonians can profit from stretching history a bit—or even out of all recognition—they will also do that. It is a tradition as old as the city itself. Read about that in this book's first chapter.

If New York City is the Big Apple, New Orleans the Big Easy and Chicago the City of Broad Shoulders, then Houston is the City of Big Ideas. From the founding of Houston, the growth of cotton and the refining of petroleum to advancements in the medical industry, the development of its inland port and its tenure as Space City, all of Houston's big ideas were embraced and adopted by its citizens. With all of this innovation, is it surprising that Houston's past vanishes and gets forgotten, including its landmarks?

This book presents the story behind fifteen of Houston's past landmarks that are linked by modern obscurity. Some involve transportation, and others involve industry. Some of them are landmark buildings that were wiped away by progress, vanished places where people went for entertainment. Houston is filled with buildings that were once landmarks, places every Houstonian knew at one time but are now forgotten. Often, the events that occurred in these forgotten places are still remembered while the actual sites are shrouded in mysteries. The places mentioned in this book include the actual site of the first steamboat landing in Houston and the location of the Twin Sisters, two cannons that helped Texas gain its independence from Mexico. In other cases, while the locations of some of these places are known, their historic significance has been forgotten. These places include NASA's first Houston headquarters building, the site of the nation's first public television station, the location where the world's first shipping container landed and the Houston grocery store that led to the collapse of the Soviet Union. For a moment, consider Houston's cotton industry. It dominated Houston's economy for two generations, but today, it has all but disappeared. The Cotton Exchange, which was once the beating economic heart of Houston, has so thoroughly vanished that it is now largely remembered for just one of its buildings.

Some of the locations in this book were places that every Houstonian knew about or used back when they were famous. These locations include the Galveston–Houston Electric Railroad, the Jefferson Davis Charity Hospital and the Goodyear Blimp Base north of Houston. You could not miss them when they were around. Other locations in this book are places where Houstonians sought entertainment. Some of these places include Buff's Stadium, Gilley's Nightclub and AstroWorld, and they were famous attractions. Folks who did not visit these places regularly would pass them. Even after these locations closed, memories of them were cherished for years. Now, they have been gone for so long that they are largely forgotten. This book also includes the story of a rich man's mansion that was only sort of famous because it was that rich man's mansion. It would have been completely forgotten if it had just been that, but the West Mansion, James M. West's spectacular summer home on Clear Lake, became famous when it served as the home of the Lunar and Planetary Institute. The mansion was such an incongruous location for a scientific research center.

All of these stories are weird, funny, sad and, I hope, captivating. They should bring light to some of the forgotten yet fascinating corners of the Greater Houston–Galveston Metropolitan Area. The tales wander from Galveston to Spring and from Pasadena to Houston's west side.

If you enjoy the stories in the book and want more, do these two things:

1. Buy a copy of this book. Buy extra copies for yourself and your friends and relations—or even acquaintances. If enough copies sell, the publisher will want sequels. (They always do.)
2. If you know of a vanished Houston landmark that was neglected by this book, let me know. When I get fifteen suitable subjects, I will write *More Vanished Houston Landmarks*. I have a few right now. Remember the terra-cotta army replica that was overrun by the Grand Parkway? Did you know the first capitol building for the Republic of Texas stood where the Rice Hotel stands today? I have more.

A POINT BEFORE WE GET STARTED: A Texian was an individual that claimed allegiance to the Republic of Texas or Mexican Colonial Texas. A Texan is an individual that claimed allegiance to the State of Texas, whether the state belonged to the United States of America or to the Confederate States of America. Until Texas joined the Union in 1845, its inhabitants called themselves Texians. After that, they became Texans.

1.

THE PERIPATETIC ALLEN'S LANDING

One of the most cherished spots in Houston is Allen's Landing. This park on the south bank of Buffalo Bayou, where it meets White Oak Bayou, marks the spot where the steamboat *Laura* made its first landing at the new city of Houston on January 27, 1837, opening the port for business. Even the Handbook of Texas gives Allen's Landing the status of being the spot where *Laura* first docked. Today, the city of Houston possesses one of the largest seaports in the United States, which makes the *Laura*'s arrival a "Plymouth Rock" moment—one where the course of history changed for the better. On its webpage, the Buffalo Bayou Partnership proclaims Allen's Landing as Houston's founding place and as "Houston's most significant and historic site." Make no mistake, Allen's Landing deserves the title of Houston's original port, but was it really Houston's "Plymouth Rock," the site of *Laura*'s first landing? The answer is a definite maybe. Untangling truth from myth requires a trip to the past, to the story of Houston's founding.

John and Augustus Allen were brothers and land speculators originally from New York. Augustus had briefly been a mathematics professor at the Polytechnic Institute at Chittenango, New York. By 1833, they were both in Louisiana considering the opportunities that were available to them in Texas. In 1836, shortly after the Texas War of Independence, the two were in Galveston, thinking about where to set up a city. Their plan was similar to the one used by Texas subdivision developers today: secure a title to a plot of land, divide it into lots after surveying a grid of streets, promote the development, sell the lots and get rich. Today's developers have to pave streets, set up utilities, provide sidewalks and construct houses and commercial buildings, but back in 1836, things were simpler. There were no electric easements to worry about, water and sewer lines were all wells that were dug by the landowner and streets were often just graded dirt and cleared pathways. Back then, just as today, the three keys to a successful development were location, location and location. You could put up a town anywhere, but people would not come to that town to buy lots unless they had a good reason to.

Galveston Island originally attracted them because it was a natural seaport and was the best location for carrying cargo out of the newly born Republic of Texas. It was the only location on the Texas coast that offered an anchorage inside the coastal barrier islands with a deep-water channel leading to it. These features protect ships from the storms that are kicked up in the Gulf of Mexico. Before the railroad, most goods traveled by water; the only alternative was to transport goods in wagons drawn by animals. Setting up a city on Galveston Island would have set the brothers on a path to wealth. However, when they arrived, they discovered that others had already had the same idea and secured a title to 4,605 acres of land on the island that would become the City of Galveston. While John and Augustus did invest in the Galveston City Company, they wanted to be more than junior partners. They wanted their own city.

They still wanted to establish a town on a waterway. Goods had to get to Texas's interior somehow, which meant they had to travel along Texas's rivers. Only bulk goods, like hides and cotton, could be transported commercially by wagon for about thirty miles. Shipping much more than that in addition to the cost of the fodder that it took to feed the livestock pulling the wagons would literally eat the profits. Everyone in Texas's interior wanted to cart their produce to the nearest river and load it onto barges or the new steamboats for shipment to a seaport. The main rivers that feed into Galveston Bay are the Trinity River, the San Jacinto River and Buffalo Bayou. In 1836, Texas's most developed area was to the west and north of the present-day city of Houston. Most goods that were shipped from that area took the Brazos River to Velasco. The modern-day city is at the mouth of the Brazos, an open roadstead that offers no shelter from Gulf storms.

There was a river port on Buffalo Bayou that offered an obvious route to Galveston's sheltered harbor, bypassing Velasco. The ideal spot for such a town was the head of navigation—the farthest point above the mouth of Buffalo Bayou that could be reached by steamboats. The problem was that

In 1837, when Francis Lubbock and friends borrowed the *Laura* to row past Buffalo Bayou to White Oak Bayou, Houston looked similar to this image, with a snag-choked shore and trees hanging over the river. *Author's collection.*

the idea to place a town on this piece of land had been just as obvious as the notion that Galveston Island would make a great place for a seaport. Nearly a dozen other empresarios had tried their hand at starting a river port on Buffalo Bayou before the Allen brothers arrived. Not all of them got their projects launched, but by 1836, there were already eight ports on Buffalo Bayou, starting with Lynchburg, where Buffalo Bayou ended, and

It took three days for the *Laura* to travel the five miles between Harrisburg and Houston. While legend holds that it landed at the foot of Main Street, the boat most likely stopped at the first street it recognized—either Lamar or Austin, as shown on this map. *Courtesy of the Houston Maritime Museum.*

proceeding west to New Washington, Powhattan, Scottsburg, Louisville, San Jacinto, Hamilton and, finally, Harrisburg. However, with the exception of Lynchburg, New Washington and Harrisburg, these were all notional cities. Given the competition, the Allens needed an edge; they had to set up their city at the head of navigation. The problem with this plan was that Harrisburg was already at the head of navigation—the spot was taken. So, the Allens' next move was to try to buy Harrisburg.

When Harrisburg's founder died in 1929, the Allens thought the town might be available to purchase. However, the title to the town was tied up in an inheritance squabble, and by 1836, the legal battle was still going strong. Balked, the Allens tried something audacious: they redefined the location of the head of navigation for Buffalo Bayou. Unclaimed land was available five miles upriver from Harrisburg, where White Oak Bayou flows into Buffalo Bayou. The brothers declared that piece of land was the true head of navigation of Buffalo Bayou and claimed the intersection of White Oak and Buffalo Bayous offered a natural turning basin. After they bought land there in August 1836, the Allens platted a new town on the land and placed Main Street right at the intersection of the two bayous.

In the typical style of land developers, they gave the town a captivating name: Houston, after the Republic of Texas's biggest hero, Sam Houston. Houston was Texas's George Washington; he was the commander of the victorious Texian army during the Republic's war for independence and the first president of the Republic. Furthermore, the brothers donated some of their town's land for the Republic's capitol building. Their offer was accepted by a cash-strapped Texian legislature, making Houston the capital as well as an essential port.

Claiming that Houston, rather than Harrisburg, was Buffalo Bayou's head of navigation could charitably be called Texas brag. Buffalo Bayou, between Houston and Harrisburg, was deep enough for the steamboats of the day, but it was narrow and twisting. The stretch could be dredged, widened and straightened out enough to make it reasonably navigable, but all of that would take money that the Allens did not have in 1836. The improvement of the five-mile stretch would have left Houston only fifteen miles east of the Brazos agricultural area and just thirty-five miles from San Filipe de Austin, the oldest Anglo colony in Texas. Five miles significantly cut the journey from the Brazos—if Houston really was head of navigation. Skeptics abounded, however; many wondered whether the brothers were

For many years, the foot of Main Street was Houston's main wharf. This picture shows how it would have appeared in the years before the Civil War. *Courtesy of the University of Houston Digital Archive Library.*

stretching the truth. Because of this doubt, the Allens had to demonstrate that they could get a steamboat to Houston.

The brothers chartered the steamboat *Laura* for the trip to Houston. At 65 feet long, the *Laura* was the smallest steamboat on the Texas rivers at the time. The steamboat departed from Galveston in early January 1837. Aboard the boat was John Allen, Mosely Baker (a San Jacinto hero), Benjamin C. Franklin (a Texas lawyer—not the founding father) and Francis Lubbock (a future Texas governor). It took the crew only a few days to reach Harrisburg, and they spent much of that time trying to free the boat after it was grounded in Galveston Bay. The final five miles of their journey consumed three days, as the boat only averaged 367 feet per hour. It was the first time a steamboat had ever traveled that stretch of Buffalo Bayou, so the crew spent a lot of time clearing the bayou of obstructions. Removing snags and heaving logs out of the bayou proved an all-hands-on-deck operation. The *Laura* was tied up each night while the passengers went ashore to party.

The brothers began selling lots in Houston on January 19, a day chosen because the *Laura* was supposed to have reached the town by then. Lubbock and some of the other crew members got impatient with the steamboat's slow progress, so they borrowed the *Laura*'s yawl and went up Buffalo Bayou seeking Houston. Lubbock later wrote of the adventure:

> *So little evidence could we see of a landing that we passed by the site and ran into White Oak Bayou, only realizing that we must have passed the city when we struck in the brush. We then backed down the bayou, and by close observation, discovered a road or street laid off from the water's edge. Upon landing, we found stakes and footprints, indicating that we were in the town tract.*

A few days later, the *Laura* finally arrived in Houston. No one really knows the exact date of the *Laura*'s landing, but the Handbook of Texas marks it as January 27. However, nineteenth-century historians claimed the date was January 22. Whether or not the *Laura* was tied up at Allen's Landing— today's foot of Main Street—is equally uncertain, but in my opinion, it is doubtful that the boat landed there. Lubbock's account says that the fork of White Oak and Buffalo Bayous was easy to miss. Houston itself only consisted of surveyors' stakes and muddy roads; there were no buildings in town, only a few tents, which were not within sight of the river.

The original layout of Houston shows Main Street in the center of eleven streets that were perpendicular to Buffalo Bayou. To the east of Main

Street were Fannin, San Jacinto, Carolina, Austin and Lamar (today's La Branch) Streets. The *Laura* had already spent three days battling the five miles between Harrisburg and Houston, so rather than struggle another few hundred yards to Main Street, it is much more likely that the captain of the *Laura* declared victory at the first set of surveyor's stakes he saw and tied up there. Why would he have risked hitting a snag trying to find Main Street? So, where did the Allens land? Pick a spot. All the streets between Main and Lamar Streets were, at the time, just mud patches marked by stakes. While it is sentimental to think that the *Laura* landed at today's Allen's Landing, one can make just as good of an argument that the boat landed at Lamar, or any of the other streets that led up to Main Street.

In the 1890s, the Port of Houston began moving downstream from its Main Street location. Plans were in hand to transform Houston into a major seaport, and since it would have been too difficult to dredge the bayou to a depth of twenty-five feet all the way to Main Street, a more practical spot for the terminus of the Houston Ship Channel was chosen. Its new location was five miles downstream from Main Street, where Harrisburg—long ago absorbed into Houston—was located.

The area on Main Street only became Allen's Landing in the 1960s, when the commercial port departed downstream and the waterfront in downtown Houston devolved into an unattractive dump. The Houston Chamber of Commerce wanted to revitalize the neglected area of downtown and helped spearhead an effort to build a park there in celebration of Houston's maritime heritage. Charlie Lansden, the then-director of the chamber's Community

Allen's Landing as it appears today. It is a cherished park in the middle of downtown Houston, at the meeting point of Main Street and Buffalo Bayou—the spot that made Houston. *Photograph by author.*

Betterment Division dubbed that section of Buffalo Bayou Allen's Landing as a marketing ploy. Allen's Landing sounded more interesting than "The Foot of Main Street," "Old Port" or something that was more historically accurate. Lansden's tactic worked, and the two-acre park was dedicated as Allen's Landing Memorial Park in 1967. The area was transformed from a blighted neighborhood of the 1960s to the Houston treasure today; it helped Houston rediscover and embrace its maritime heritage.

Whether or not the *Laura* landed there, the corner of Main and Water Streets (today's Allen's Landing) is historically significant, as it was the site of the original Port of Houston. Even if *Laura* tied up somewhere else in January 1837, Houston's first wharves were built at the foot of Main Street shortly after the boat's famous trip. Over time, Buffalo Bayou was deepened and widened, with a ten-foot-deep channel that reached the foot of Main Street. For the next sixty years, the foot of Main Street was the heart of Houston's port district. The port was the reason for Houston's existence and remains a major industry in the city today—it should be celebrated. Today, Allen's Landing is one of the trendier spots in Houston's waterfront district and is known for its annual spring festival. A replica of the original port has been built in the park. It is one of the jewels of central Houston and is surrounded by the University of Houston–Downtown.

2.

THE LOST SISTERS

The Battle of San Jacinto settled the outcome of the Texas War of Independence and, as a result, decided the eventual shape of the United States. Roughly 2,100 men—some 900 Texians and 1,300 Mexicans—fought on marshy prairie near the junction of Buffalo Bayou and the San Jacinto River on April 21, 1836. The Texian army charged across the field at 4:30 p.m. and caught the Mexican army napping. Twenty minutes later, the Mexican army routed and fled the field, and the Texians eventually captured Santa Anna de Lopez, the Mexican commander and president. Santa Anna eventually traded the independence of Texas for his own freedom, thus concluding the new Texas Republic's struggle to gain independence from Mexico.

Every April, a reenactment of the Battle of San Jacinto is held at Battleground Park, where the battle was fought. If you have ever attended a reenactment, you probably watched the artillery duel that precedes each battle. The Texians fire two cannons, and the Mexicans respond with one. The two Texian cannons at the battle were called the Twin Sisters. The Texas War of Independence generated tremendous support throughout the United States. In Cincinnati, Ohio, the citizens raised funds to cast two cannons that they later donated to the Texian forces. The resulting iron smoothbores were cast at the foundry of Greenwood and Webb in Cincinnati, Ohio.

Little is known about the guns, and they have been variously described as four-pounders and six-pounders; their weight and dimensions are unknown. Some sources even claim the guns were made of brass, which is unlikely

Reenactors fire a replica of one of the Twin Sisters cannons at the annual San Jacinto Day reenactment of the battle that won Texas's independence. *Photograph by author.*

since Greenwood and Webb was an iron foundry. Greenwood and Webb was still in business in the 1980s, when some Texans wanted replicas of the guns made for the 1986 Texas sesquicentennial. Alas, time had worked its vanishing act, and all of the drawings and plans the foundry had for the Twin Sisters had disappeared by then. The only fact about the cannons that is known for certain is that they arrived in Texas in time for the Battle of San Jacinto and helped secure the Texian victory. The cannons are thought to still be in Houston, but no one knows where. In the days of the Republic prior to the Civil War, Texians and Texans did not worry about paperwork, so the trail of the two cannons quickly became blurred. They were known to have been in Austin in 1842 to protect the capital. The cannons then went to the Texas frontier with troops who raided Mexican troops and occupied San Antonio. After this, things get fuzzy.

The most common tale about the cannons is that they, along with the rest of the property of the Republic of Texas's army and navy, were turned over to the United States Army when Texas joined the Union in 1845. The U.S. Army was supposed to ship them to the Baton Rouge armory for storage. Eventually, the origins of the guns were forgotten, and they became viewed as unnecessary ordnance taking up valuable armory space. In the late 1850s, it is said that the guns were sold as scrap iron to a foundry in Baton Rouge.

The Handbook of Texas, however, insists that the Twin Sisters remained in Austin for another twenty years. The website states that the guns shipped to Baton Rouge were two six-pounders that were acquired in 1836 by Thomas Jefferson Chambers and turned over to the Republic. The secession government of Texas was not as certain as the Handbook of Texas that the guns sent to Baton Rouge were the Chambers guns. The government of Texas sent a delegation to Louisiana to recover the guns, which it believed were the authentic Twin Sisters. The delegates discovered that the guns were gone, sold to a foundry in Baton Rouge as scrap. Business must have been slow at that foundry, because when the delegates checked, one of the guns was still there, awaiting its turn in the smelter. The second gun had been sold to a private citizen in Iberville Parish as a lawn ornament. The State of Louisiana, in a show of solidarity with Texas, repurchased the cannons, refurbished them and mounted them on new carriages. On each carriage, Louisiana attached a brass plaque, proclaiming each gun to be one of the Twin Sisters and outlining the history of the guns. They were back in Texas by San Jacinto Day 1861, and a letter appeared in the April 20, 1861 edition of the *State Gazette* claiming the cannons had arrived in Galveston. Regardless of whether it was the Twin Sisters or the Chambers guns that were sent to Baton Rouge, these two mounted cannons became sacred symbols of Texas independence and important pieces of Texas's heritage.

From there, the trail of the cannons again becomes blurry. They may or may not have been used at the Battle of Galveston on New Year's Eve 1863. They may have also been used in 1862 at the invasion of New Mexico, where it is said that one of the guns was lost. It is known that the guns were sent to Brownsville in 1864 to beef up the Confederate defenses at the abandoned Fort Brown after Robert A. Lee surrendered in Virginia. The cannons' last definitive appearance was recorded in a report written on November 30, 1863, which stated they were in Austin "in poor condition."

Once the United States reoccupied Texas in 1865, the army rounded up Confederate ordnance in the state. Guns throughout Texas, including the Twin Sisters, were shipped to Houston for shipment to the North. M.A. Sweetman was a Union soldier in the 114th Ohio Volunteer Regiment and

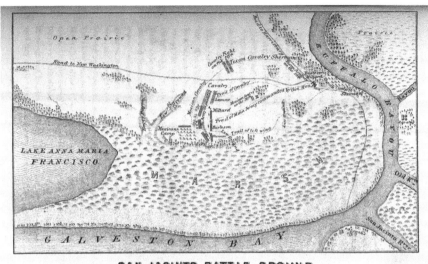

SAN JACINTO BATTLE-GROUND.

A nineteenth-century map of the San Jacinto battlefield. The location of the Twin Sisters at the start and finish of the battle can be seen at either end of the dashed line marked "Trail of Main Army commanded by Gen. Houston." *Author's collection.*

was on garrison duty in Houston in July 1865. He reported seeing two six-pound cannons in Houston's Market Square on July 30. He claimed that the guns' carriages had brass plaques proclaiming that they were the the Twin Sisters that had been presented by the state of Louisiana to the State of Texas on March 4, 1861.

Were the guns sent north and melted down? Maybe—then again, maybe not. Henry North Graves claimed the guns had a different fate. In August 1865, Graves was returning home from the war with his servant and four fellow veterans from his unit. While traveling from Galveston to Houston, the group saw the captive cannons, along with other Confederate artillery, in a trackside artillery park in nearby Harrisburg, Texas, waiting to be sent north for scrapping. According to Graves, the group snuck into the artillery park during the night and rolled the Twin Sisters to a nearby patch of woods. By the banks of Brays Bayou, Graves said the group dug a hole that was three feet deep and buried the gun barrels in it. Next, he said the group disposed of the guns' carriages. Graves claimed they burned them, but a fire would have attracted attention. Brays Bayou was close by, so they may have just tipped them in there.

The grouped hoped to someday recover the cannons. They marked the trees, noted landmarks and went home to wait. It took a while for "someday" to come. Graves first tried to locate the guns on his own in 1895. In 1905, the three surviving men from the party, including Graves, returned to the railroad yard to search for the guns. It was safe to recover them, but they could not find them. The city had changed over forty years; streets had been relayed, buildings had been torn down, railroad lines had moved and Brays Bayou had shifted. The three found some of their old marks, but they could not find the buried guns.

Graves went public with his story about the Twin Sisters. The *Houston Chronicle* persuaded Graves to return to Houston in 1920 to search again, but he had no luck. Since then, searching for the guns has become a cottage industry in Houston, but they have yet to be found. If Graves's story is accurate, the Twin Sisters are somewhere near Brays Bayou, near the old town of Harrisburg, perhaps one half mile west of the modern Interstate 610 East Loop.

However, Graves's story could just be a story. Going against his account are the physical capabilities the men would have needed to accomplish the heist. The returning veterans were in poor shape; they had been ill-fed for months, and one man had measles. According to Graves, these six men would have had to sneak a cannon that weighed at least 350 (more likely 900) pounds out of a guarded area. Next, they would have

The Twin Sisters were reported to have been at several battles in Texas during the American Civil War. This image shows where the guns were said to have assisted recapture of the port in Brownsville, Texas. *Courtesy of the Library of Congress.*

had to roll the cannon across four football fields' worth of boggy and muddy ground before finally burying it three feet deep in the swamp. They allegedly did all of these things not once but twice, and they did them without being detected. It would have been a lot of work for six sick men to do in one night, but stranger things have happened. It is likely that the yard was not well guarded—if it was even guarded at all. While the rifles that were stored there may have been useful to criminals, cannons were not—even light ones like the Twin Sisters. Since the war was over, it is also plausible that the Union troops occupying Texas did not think anyone would be interested in spiriting the heavy guns away from the trackside park where they were stored. What a criminal have done with them anyway—use them in a bank heist?

One of the brass plaques from the cannons' carriages did, however, later turn up in New York, where it was presented to Governor Pat Neff in 1924. Today, the plaque is at Baylor University's Mayborn Museum. If the cannons had been burned or tipped into Brays Bayou in 1865, how did they end up in New York? Did Graves and his buddies really bury the guns, or was this something they wished they had done? Did the survivors eventually convince themselves that something they had talked about doing—something they felt they should have done—had really happened? Old soldiers do that sometimes. Regardless of whether they actually buried the cannons or simply wanted to bury them, Graves and his buddies believed that they had buried the guns. Why else would they have made the return trips to look for them?

It is possible that the men did bury some cannon that day. It is also possible that they buried the real Twin Sisters. If the two guns presented to Texas by Louisiana were really the Chambers guns, as the Handbook of Texas asserts, then the plaques were placed on the wrong cannons before they were shipped north. Another possibility suggested by the Handbook of Texas is that Graves and his company buried two cannons that were originally from the schooner *Cayuga*. These cannons were also shipped north with the rest of the Confederate ordnance. Few people knew what the Twin Sisters actually looked like, so it would have been easy to confuse the guns.

In the late 1920s, warehouses and small industrial shops sprang up around the supposed burial site of the guns. The land was either dug up to provide foundations for warehouses or graded and paved over. During World War II, the wooded bayou banks were transformed into a major part of the Arsenal of Democracy. Starting in 1940, shipyards, chemical

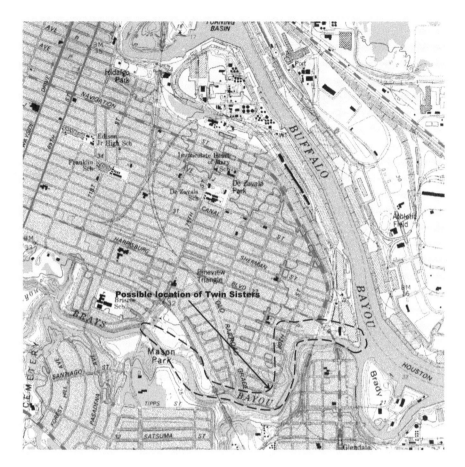

According to Henry North Graves, he and his buddies buried the guns somewhere within the dashed area of the map. Extensive construction in the area since the 1930s makes it unlikely that the guns are still there—even if they once were. This topographic map was made in the 1980s. *Author's collection.*

and petroleum plants and tank farms sprouted up like mushrooms along Buffalo Bayou and the connecting bayous. Harrisburg continued to be transformed by heavy industry after the war ended in 1945. Today, Harrisburg has been absorbed into Houston, and the land where the guns were reportedly buried is now an industrial area.

The guns may have been buried in the soil that was dumped on the banks of Brays Bayou when it was deepened and straightened. Or perhaps they were unearthed during the long-ago construction of the terminal and tank farm and sent into a spoil field unnoticed. Houston was not big on historical preservation in the early and middle parts of the twentieth century, so it's possible a shovel or bulldozer operator plowed up the cannons, figured they were just some old iron pipes and either reburied them or dumped them into a dump truck to be hauled away. Or perhaps Graves's account was just an old soldier's story and the cannons were never there to begin with. Who knows, maybe while tramping down the bank of Brays Bayou you will pass within yards of the two most famous guns in Texas history.

3.

WHEN COTTON WAS KING IN HOUSTON

Sometimes, it is not a landmark object or building that disappears but a landmark organization. Such is the case of the Houston Cotton Exchange and Board of Trade—not the 1884 Cotton Exchange Building or the second building that was used to house the organization in 1924—but the organization that built both.

The 1884 building remains a beloved Houston landmark and is a rare piece of nineteenth-century Houston history that was preserved and cherished. It has been called the most beautiful building in Houston. Today, it houses a candy store and a wine and whiskey bar. Visitors can test for themselves to see if candy is dandy or liquor is quicker. The 1924 building at 1300 Prairie Street is also still in use and is now a county government office building. Its original purpose, along with the cotton exchange it once housed, is largely forgotten. Domestic abuse, not cotton trading, is the building's focus today, as it houses the Harris County Domestic Relations Office.

The Cotton Exchange, which gave rise to both buildings, was once as integral a part of Houston's identity as the Johnson Space Center and the petrochemical industry are today. The Houston Cotton Exchange and Board of Trade existed for just over one hundred years. For at least fifty of those years, it dominated Houston's economic sphere. Yet, just a century after the apex of its influence, the Cotton Exchange is almost completely forgotten. If you search "Houston Cotton Exchange" online, your hits will discuss the 1884 building and only mention the organization in passing.

The Trading Floor

The trading floor of the Houston Cotton Exchange was the heart of Houston's economy for over fifty years. *Author's collection.*

For the first century of Houston's history, the combination of cotton and transportation was the reason for the city's existence. The growth of the cotton industry in Texas was the reason the Allen Brothers declared Houston to be Buffalo Bayou's head of navigation. Cotton was the main cash crop of the Brazos River bottomlands, and from there, it streamed into Houston. Originally, cotton was moved by long wagon trains laden with the year's crop. Once the wagons reached Houston, the crop would be loaded onto barges and riverboats at the foot of Main Street. From there, the cotton would travel to Galveston or Bolivar Roads, where it would be loaded onto ships for transport to the mills in New England and Great Britain. With the arrival of the railroad in the 1850s, cotton was shipped to the foot of Main Street in boxcars and flatcars. It was still cheaper to load the cotton onto rivercraft in Houston than to send it to Galveston by rail—at least with the primitive locomotives that were available prior to 1871. From 1837 to 1871, Houston grew rich using this system. After Houston became a seaport and the Houston Ship Channel was completed in 1871, the city even started to skip the transshipment of the cotton to Galveston and sent cargos directly to Europe.

Just how important was cotton to Houston? In 1849, Texas produced 14,500 tons of cotton, and most of that came from plantations in the Brazos

River bottomlands. By 1859, the cotton crop totaled 108,000 tons. Two-thirds of that crop left Texas through Galveston, and most of that cotton reached Galveston after being loaded onto barges and steamboats in Houston. The Civil War years saw a reduction in Texas's exportation of cotton, but Galveston remained an important cotton port. Houston served as the primary transshipment point for Texas cotton that was heading to Galveston. Due to the disruptions of the Civil War, Texas's 1869 cotton crop totaled only 88,000 tons, but by 1879, it bounced back to 201,321 tons—nearly double the crop from twenty years earlier. From then on—thanks to the new cotton plantations in Central Texas and the Texas Panhandle and the arrival of the railroads—cotton production nearly doubled every decade. Texas produced 375,000 tons of cotton in 1889 and was producing 875,000 tons annually by 1900. Cotton was white gold.

In the mid-nineteenth century, the brokers who bought the cotton were also often the merchants who sold supplies to the planters. Brokers could get rich trading cotton, but their success was dependent on factors beyond their control. Cotton trading in Texas was based on the price of cotton on the Liverpool and New York exchanges. Before the advent of the telegraph and transatlantic cable, trades were made on information that was over a month old. The price of cotton on the European and East Coast markets was not the only important factor for a cotton broker; the quality of the cotton was also critical to getting a good price. Samples had to be examined and graded according to established standards. Getting rich as a cotton trader was a like making a living as a riverboat gambler who lacked the ability to stack the cards in his favor.

Gaining information was one way brokers could shift the odds in their favor. The telegraph reached Houston in 1854 and allowed information from East Coast exchanges to reach cotton traders in Texas in a day or two. By 1870, there was a transatlantic telegraph in commercial service that allowed reports from European cotton exchanges, especially the dominant Liverpool Exchange, to reach Houston in just a few days. While telegraphs were expensive at this time, Houston cotton traders all needed this information. They also needed a uniform grading system for cotton and information about the reliability and honesty of their buyers and sellers. Individuals in the cotton industry began to agree that it made sense to divide the cost of telegraphs and grading among a pool of cotton brokers and traders. By the late 1860s, the trading volume of cotton was growing to the point that a broker could lose his fortune in one bad deal. By breaking up their sales into smaller, more numerous trades, brokers

The *Houston Post* ran this political cartoon to show the magnitude of Houston's cotton industry and the city's pride in it. Over 2.5 million five-hundred-pound bales went through Houston in 1899. *Courtesy of the Houston Maritime Museum.*

hedged their investments against failure. This system worked better when brokers worked with partners in joint deals. Cooperation was the key to both increased profits and decreased risk.

On the evening of May 15, 1874, a group of Houston merchants and cotton brokers met to organize the Houston Board of Trade. They agreed to a $5 initiation fee and dues of $1 per month (which is approximately equivalent to $1,000 and $200, respectively, today). They also appointed a committee to draw up a constitution and bylaws for their new organization, and the committee returned its report on June 12. The organization was renamed the Houston Cotton Exchange and Board of Trade, and a president, two vice-presidents and a ten-member board of directors were elected. After that, the Houston Cotton Exchange was off and running. Part of the Cotton Exchange's purpose was its trading floor—a place where brokers could exchange trading information—called Perkins Hall. The Exchange also leased part of Perkins Hall to Pilot's Opera House to serve as its venue.

The initial Exchange facilities were sparse and only had one small bulletin board on which quotes were posted. These quotes came in by telegraph, but in the late 1870s, high telegraph word rates kept telegraphic traffic low. At that time, price quotes only came from the St. Louis Commodity Exchange, so there were relatively few notices available to be posted. The Cotton Exchange's first secretary, George Kidd, was the business editor of a local newspaper and supplemented the telegraphs with items from his paper. As telegraphy matured and rates dropped, more information was posted. The completion of the railroad connections between Houston and St. Louis increased trade in Texas, so more space was needed. Additionally, Houston's other theater burned down, which meant the Pilot's Opera House began hosting more performances and also needed more space.

In 1882, members of the exchange's board began to discuss purchasing its own building. The idea became reality in 1883, and construction on the building began in June 1884. The completed building, a three-story, red brick Victorian Renaissance Revival building was completed in November 1884. The new, larger trading floor was located on the third story of the building. It was later moved to the first floor when the building was remodeled to include a fourth floor. This building served the exchange for forty years, and during that time, the Houston Cotton Exchange saw continuous rapid growth. In the 1883–84 cotton season, 521,909 bales (or 130,000 tons) of cotton moved through the Houston Cotton Exchange, which was over one-third of the cotton grown in Texas that season. By 1900, Houston handled 2.5 million bales of cotton, and while this was a smaller percentage of Texas's cotton crop, it represented a 500 percent increase in the amount cotton moving through Houston. The board on the trading floor began to list not only the St. Louis exchange prices but also the prices from the New Orleans, New York, and Liverpool exchanges.

The transformation of Houston from a river port to a seaport accelerated with the growth and influence of the Cotton Exchange. Houston's evolution started with the dredging of a nine-foot channel to the junction of the Sims and Buffalo Bayous in 1876 and ended with the completion of the Houston Ship Channel in 1914. The channel was a twenty-five-foot-deep waterway that stretched from the mouth of Galveston Bay to today's Turning Basin.

By 1924, the Houston Cotton Exchange had badly outgrown its 1884 building and built a new seventeen-story Cotton Exchange Building to replace it. *Author's collection.*

Another increase in trading forced the exchange to abandon its chamber of commerce functions, and by 1900, the organization was exclusively focused on cotton trading. The exchange regularly celebrated the arrival of Texas's first cotton bale of each season by ceremoniously auctioning it off. It also celebrated the arrival of each season's millionth bale, when it occurred, in the same way. Between 1900 and 1925, the Houston Cotton Exchange continued to grow as Texas's cotton industry reached maturity. Between 1900 and 1928, Texas regularly exceeded the amount of cotton that was grown (870,000 tons) in 1900. During several seasons, the cotton crop reached or exceeded 1.0 million tons, with the record of 1.4 million tons produced in 1928. However, there were also years when cotton production was well below the amount from 1900. In 1921, a mere 525,000 tons of cotton was delivered. Yet, during the good and bad years, the percentage of the Texas crop moving through Houston was high; it was never below one-third. In 1924, 61 percent of the cotton grown in Texas passed through Houston.

By 1900, the exchange's membership exceeded one hundred people, and by 1920, the Houston Cotton Exchange had nearly two hundred dues-paying members. By 1922, with the exchange's fiftieth anniversary just two years away, the members voted to build a new exchange building—one that could house a larger trading floor, more sample rooms for grading cotton and enough offices to house the captains of Houston's cotton industry. The building's construction was completed in 1924. The trading floor, along with the offices of the exchange's officers and director were placed on the sixteenth floor. The first floor was reserved for shops that offered services that were of interest to traders, including those of a barber. On the fourteen floors between them were the sample rooms and business offices of those who were involved in shipping cotton, including traders, shipping and railroad agents and representatives of the warehouses and compresses. The building was perfect for the organization when it was completed, and perhaps this should have been a warning. One of Parkinson's laws states that when an organization finally has a building that fits its needs, it is heading toward obsolescence. This proved to be true for the Houston Cotton Exchange. The opening of the building marked the high and midpoints of the exchange's existence.

Like a rocket that was exhausting its fuel, the exchange's trading volumes kept growing until 1929. The Great Depression had surprisingly little to do with the exchange's decline. Cotton shipments declined during some years of the 1930s, but during others, the annual shipments exceeded the

Today, the old 1884 Cotton Exchange Building has been restored and is considered a symbol of Houston's heritage and the city's resolve to preserve its history. It now houses a candy store and a wine and whiskey bar. *Courtesy of the Library of Congress.*

numbers of the 1920s. Most of the exchange's decline has been blamed on cotton's declining relative importance to other Houston exports, particularly petroleum. Black gold replaced white gold. An article from the 1951 issue of the Houston Port Authority's *Port Magazine* stated, "A year in which cotton exports failed to reach a million bales would be exceptional." Given that the port routinely shipped two to five times that volume during the 1920s and 1930s, the article was putting a positive spin on bad news.

Synthetic materials began to replace cotton in the 1950s and 1960s. And the Houston Cotton Exchange lost influence and relevance throughout the decades. It celebrated its centennial in 1974 to little fanfare. Ironically, the 1884 building had been restored the previous year and was on its way to being celebrated as a symbol of the preservation of Houston's history. Sometime during the 1970s—almost unnoticed—the Houston Cotton Exchange disposed of its assets and dissolved. One of its last acts was to transfer its archives to the Houston Public Library's Houston Metropolitan Research Center, a task it completed in 1978.

4.

ELECTRIC RIDE IN VIEW

Houston's METRORail, a street-level electric rail system, opened in
2004. Riders move silently and swiftly through Houston on trains
powered by electricity. Many of Houston's citizens think it is the
latest and greatest thing in ground transportation. Yet, METRORail was not
Houston's first encounter with electric rail transportation. Nearly a century
earlier, on November 23, 1911, the Galveston–Houston Electric Railway—
better known as the Galveston–Houston Interurban—opened for operation.

For its time, the Galveston–Houston Interurban was an engineering
marvel. It linked Houston and Galveston with 50.5 miles of track. Between
Park Place and Virginia Point—for 34.0 miles—the track ran in a straight
line. With the exception of a bridge, where the track passed over the Santa
Fe railroad near Texas City Junction, the maximum grade was 0.5 percent—
or 1 foot of elevation for every 200 feet of track. The track started at Texas
Avenue and Smith Street in Houston and ended in Galveston at Twenty-First
Street (Kemper Avenue), between Postoffice and Church Streets. Between
Houston and Galveston, the track had stops in South Houston, Genoa,
Webster, League City, Dickinson, La Marque, Texas City Junction (just west
of Texas City) and Virginia Point. Between the Houston and South Houston
stations, a passenger could flag down the train at Belt Junction, Kensington,
Brookline and Park Place. Passengers could also board and exit at Power
Plant (between Webster and League City), Oleander (between Dickinson and
La Marque) and Oyster (between Virginia Point and Galveston).In 1912, the
fare for the Galveston–Houston Interurban was $1.50 for a one-way trip and

The logo of the Galveston–Houston Electric Railroad. It was also known as the Galveston–Houston Interurban. Its slogan was "speed with safety." Their trains traveled at up to sixty miles per hour. *Author's collection.*

$2.40 round trip. (The railway also sold $1.95 round-trip weekend excursion tickets.) The trains were powered by three dedicated electric generation plants: a three-thousand-kilowatt plant just north of Clear Creek and two three-hundred-kilowatt plants at substations next to the South Houston and La Marque stations.

The Galveston–Houston Interurban was built for speed. Its straight track and low grade allowed the trains to reach sixty miles per hour. In 1925 and 1926, the railway took first place in *Electric Traction Magazine*'s speed contest, winning the title of the Fastest Interurban in the United States. Locals left Houston and Galveston on the railway every hour between 5:00 a.m. and 10:00 p.m. (the railway's final departure was at 11:20 p.m.) and would arrive at the other end of the line one hundred minutes later. The express nonstops—the Galveston Flyer that traveled from Houston to Galveston and the Houston Rocket that traveled from Galveston to Houston—took only seventy-five minutes to complete the trip. The cars hummed along—literally as well as figuratively. The trains made no throaty internal combustion growls; instead, they gave an electric hum as they seemingly glided down the track. The hums occasionally punctuated by clicks as the wheels passed from one rail to the next. The route was single-track, except for one mile of passing track that was scattered along the route and 1,200 feet of siding at various stations that allowed trains to pass while passengers and goods were loaded and unloaded. The railway was not intended to remain single-track; the right of way that was purchased by the owners was one hundred feet wide, which would allow for a second track to be added when it was required.

While today's mass transit is government-subsidized, government-funded and government-built, the Galveston–Houston Electric Railway Company was organized as a for-profit corporation. Chartered on March 2, 1905, the railway was funded by a group of Houston businessmen. Stone and Webster Engineering (a Boston company) took charge of its construction in 1908, but construction did not begin until March 1910. The delay was partially due to negotiations related to building a causeway that would link Galveston Island to the mainland. A joint-use causeway—with railroad tracks, interurban tracks and a highway—was the result of these negotiations, and the Galveston-Houston Interurban paid for one-quarter of the construction costs. Once the construction started, it progressed swiftly. The last spike was driven on October 19, 1911, just nineteen months after construction started. The first train ran the line on November 23, 1911, and the Interurban opened to the public on December 5, 1911.

It would have been nice if the Interurban had become a roaring success, with a ridership and freight traffic that demanded a double-track system, but it was not. The railway conducted good business, especially in its early days, and it was certainly profitable through most of its lifetime. However, it was never Microsoft- or Facebook-level profitable; it had several problems. The railway was expensive. The $2.40 that passengers spent on a round-trip ticket is equivalent to about $65 today. In 1912, an average worker earned $750 per year, which meant a daily workday commute on the Galveston–Houston Electric Railway would have eaten up most of their year's wages.

The railway was also inconvenient to some potential users, especially those between Houston and Galveston. While the Interurban wiggled around Houston and Galveston proper, it ran in a straight line between Genoa and Virginia Point. That took passengers significantly west of League City, La Marque and Texas City. Along with Webster, these towns were the largest between Galveston and Houston at the time. To reach the nearest Interurban depot to League City from downtown League City, riders had to walk between one-half and three-quarters of a mile. Texas City was nearly five miles from the depot at Texas City Junction, which is a long walk.

The railway also had several other problems that were caused by the area's tropical weather. The 1915 Galveston Hurricane destroyed part of the track, collapsed part of the line over the causeway and damaged several cars. One car was caught on the causeway during the storm, and its conductor

A postcard showing the Texas Avenue and Smith Street terminal of the Interurban, along with one of the railcars. One-car trains were the norm, especially for the express runs. *Courtesy of the University of Houston Digital Archive Library.*

and several passengers were killed as a result. The Galveston–Houston Interurban had to pay one-quarter of the repair costs, which wiped out most of its profits that year. A second, but milder storm in 1921 burned out the motors of one car with salt spray.

Despite these setbacks, the railway did well during its first fifteen years. It added cars, began running two-car trains and added express and special trains for summer holiday traffic. Southeast Houston grew during the 1910s, which led to an increase in commuter passenger traffic between downtown Houston and the stations along the route to Park Place. The Interurban peaked in 1926 after winning the title of Fastest Interurban for the second time. The railway also had its first collision that year, when an express car hit a freight train at the Texas City Junction. Fortunately, there were no fatalities.

From there, the railway started on a long downhill slide. The Galveston–Houston Interurban helped create its own competition when it entered a partnership to build an automobile bridge over part of the Galveston Causeway. The railway was unwilling to take on the whole cost of repairing the Galveston Causeway, so this partnership probably seemed like a good idea at the time. Automobiles were still fairly uncommon, especially in the South, when the railway opened. However, owning personal automobiles became common after World War I. If a passenger owned an automobile, why would they not use it for the trip to Galveston or Houston? By the late 1920s, busses also began posing a threat to the railway. Running a bus line required little capital investment from the city; it only had to pay the cost of the vehicles, a storage barn and perhaps a depot—there was no track or power station maintenance. In 1928, the Galveston–Houston Interurban attempted to buy up the bus lines that ran between Galveston and Houston to combat the competition, but new bus lines kept popping up.

To contain costs, the railway's depots in League City, La Marque and Dickinson were shuttered and their station agents were removed in 1928. Passengers could still meet the train at those stops, but they had to buy tickets aboard the train. When the Great Depression hit, the economy was hurt, which cut the demand for travel. In the middle of the 1930s, the Galveston–Houston Interurban discontinued its special and express lines, limiting service to its hourly locals. Finally, on October 31, 1936, the Galveston–Houston Electric Railway conducted its last day of service, and its final run arrived in Galveston at 1:00 a.m. on November 1.

The Galveston–Houston Interurbandid not disappear, however; its assets, including its right-of-way, remained. The Houston Electric Company owned the Houston streetcar system and bought out the Galveston–Houston Electric Railway. Three years later, the electric company closed its electric

A stretch of track near Virginia Point. The Interurban ran straight as an arrow for more than half of its length. With no curves and almost no grade, the line was built for speed. *Courtesy of the University of Houston Digital Archive Library.*

streetcar system, ending Houston's streetcar service. The railway's cars were sold, and its property was disposed of. By inheriting the Galveston–Houston Interurban, the Houston Electric Company assumed responsibility for removing its tracks, which was expensive.

Then, while Oscar Holcombe was serving his third term as Houston's mayor, he cut a deal with Houston Electric to donate the Galveston–Houston Interurban's right-of-ways within Houston's city limits. The city took responsibility for the track, and instead of removing it, Holcombe planned to have it paved over. He felt the route would be perfect for the latest thing in transportation—a freeway. Work on the freeway, which was named the Gulf Freeway, did not start until 1948, during Holcombe's fourth term as mayor. It was completed in 1952, when it finally reached Galveston. The section from downtown Houston to the Interstate 610 loop follows the Galveston–Houston Interurban's right-of-way.

As for the rest of the track in Galveston, it was built over. The depot building and car barns were torn down and replaced by parking lots and commercial buildings. The rest of the track was removed from the right-of-way. The right-of-way was built from eighty-pound track, which meant each yard of it weighed eighty pounds. While this was light for mainline track from the middle of the twentieth century, it would have been beneficial for secondary uses. With World War II fueling an industrial boom, by 1939, the track likely was repurposed. Regardless, the track's removal left a one-hundred-foot wide, arrow-straight path available for use, and the Houston Electric had the perfect idea. The company installed an electrical transmission line, which runs from the former location of the Genoa station to Virginia Point, near where the 1912 Causeway leaves the mainland for Galveston Island. The transmission towers stand astride the old right-of-way to this day.

Today, most traces of the Galveston–Houston Electric Railway are gone. The best place to spot its remnants is along the electrical transmission line. It is easiest to find south of Loop Interstate 610. When driving along any of the roads connecting Interstate 45 to State Highway 3 (Old Galveston Road) from the Loop to Texas City, visitors will pass under the line. They can even park near the lines (it is rare to be able to park directly under them) and walk to them. Visitors can see all the way down the arrow-straight right-of-way, which is largely unchanged. Although the track has been covered by overgrown grass, it is clearly visible, especially in the sections where it was built above ground level to maintain its grade.

Other traces of the old railway still remain as well. While the League City power station is long gone, traces of it remain at the southern end of what is now a tank farm. The trestle across Clear Creek next to the station

The track right-of-way today. All of the Galveston–Houston Electric Railroad buildings have been torn down, including the depots and power plants. The right-of-way of the electric railroad is now used as an electric transmission corridor. *Photograph by author.*

was also torn down long ago, but its footings still exist under the muddy waters of Clear Creek. While driving down FM-518, League City's Main Street between Highway 3 and Interstate 45, visitors pass Interurban Street. It marks the location of League City's old Interurban Depot. While driving down Interstate 45 from Smith and Pierce to the Interstate 610 Loop, travelers pass above the old Galveston–Houston Interurban right-of-way. When it first served as a roadway, the tracks were paved over. However, it is doubtful that the tracks are still there due to the frequent rebuilding of the expressway. If you pass an electric car on the expressway, listen to it. It will echo the hum of the long-ago Galveston–Houston Interurban railcars, and maybe you will be able to imagine yourself riding in one.

5.

LET'S GO TO THE BALLPARK

When drivers travel on Loop 610 South, they pass what was once hailed as the eighth Wonder of the World—the Astrodome. It was once the home of the Houston Astros but no longer. The Astros have moved six miles north to Minute Maid Park in the heart of Houston's downtown. The Astrodome sits forlorn, abandoned and perhaps wondering if it will share the fate of its companion across the freeway—the AstroWorld amusement park.

This is not the first time that the city of Houston has abandoned a professional baseball stadium. Before the Astrodome was Buffs Stadium, an almost forgotten piece of Houston's past. The Houston Buffs were one of the city's early professional baseball teams. In 1888, the Texas League was formed, and its players were actually paid to participate—then a radical concept. Houston had one of the league's charter teams. It was called the Houston Babies because it was the last and, therefore, youngest team admitted to the league in its foundation year. The team was soon renamed the Mud Cats, a name it kept until 1894. Baseball has always been big in Houston, as it is everywhere in the United States. Between the 1870s and 1960s, it was the biggest sport in the country—America's pastime. Football displaced it from its throne just a couple of years after the first Super Bowl in January 1967. However, even today, baseball plays a big part in Houston's character. Even when Hurricane Harvey drenched Houston in 2017, the Houston Astros won that year's National League Pennant and the World Series Championship, which helped rally the community and served to mark the city's recovery.

While professional baseball is one of America's favorite sports today, it was perhaps too radical a concept in late-nineteenth-century Texas. The problem may have been that there was not enough interest in paying to see a ballgame. Or perhaps the problem was that professional baseball players in those pioneer days lacked business and entrepreneurial skills. The Mud Cats and Texas League eventually went bust and closed up shop at the end of the 1894 season. But at that point, Houston had become too taken by baseball to go without its own home team. Its baseball team was revived in 1896, this time as the Houston Buffaloes. The Houston Buffaloes won the league pennant that year, and while the team struggled over the next eight years, Houston remained proud of its team. The team's fortunes changed for the better in 1903, when it became part of the South Texas League. It became competitive, winning the league pennant in 1909, sharing a pennant with Dallas in 1910 and winning back-to-back league championships in 1914 and 1915. By then, everyone was simply calling the team the Buffs. At that time, the concept of major and minor leagues had emerged, and the Texas League was not one of the major leagues. However, it was in the top tier of the minor leagues, just one step below the majors. In 1920, major-league professional baseball was limited to sixteen teams in two major leagues. All sixteen teams were clustered in the northeast corner of the United States. St. Louis was the westernmost team's location and Washington, D.C., was home to the southernmost major-league team.

The farm system was soon developed, in which major-league teams purchased minor-league teams—including Texas League teams—to serve as feeders. Until 1920, the big leagues barred major-league teams from owning minor-league teams. In 1923, after this rule was abolished, the St. Louis Cardinals bought the controlling interest in the Buffs, making the team their finishing school. It became the first minor-league team owned by a major-league team. When the Cardinals bought the Buffs, the team was playing in West End Park on the west side of today's downtown district in the Freedman's Town section of the Fourth Ward. (Today's Pearce Elevated passes over that ballpark's former location.) The facility only seated 2,500 people, although as many as 8,300 people crowded in for one game. The Cardinals decided the park was too small for their new farm team, so in 1927, the team started constructing a new stadium on Cullen Boulevard. The site was in what was then the far southeastern outskirts of Houston, almost halfway to Pasadena.

The new stadium seated eleven thousand people, although fifteen thousand attended the opening game that was held there on April 11, 1928. At the time, it was the largest crowd that had ever attended a baseball game in Houston. Also in attendance was baseball commissioner Kenesaw Mountain Landis. He declared Buffs Stadium the "finest minor league baseball park in America." Not only did Houston's citizens turn out for its first game but so did prominent Texas politicians. Texas's governor at the time, Dan Moody, threw out the first pitch. The pitch was caught by the man who was serving as Houston's mayor, Oscar Holcombe. Acting as umpire was Houston businessman Jesse H. Jones. The Houston Buffs won the opener 7–5 against the Waco Cubs, another Texas League team. There was also a pillow fight in the stands that day, with spectators tossing seat cushions at each other. No one

WHITE, HOUSTON

Foley White was a player for the Houston Buffs in the 1910s. *Courtesy of the Library of Congress.*

knows who won that game, so it is best called a draw. Through the years, the Buffs provided Houston with some outstanding baseball games. They were league champions a dozen times between 1903 and 1958, when the team was eventually dissolved. Two Buffs teams, the 1931 and 1941 teams, are listed among the one hundred all-time greatest minor-league teams. Two Buffs players from the 1930s, Jay (Dizzy) Dean and Joe Medwick, were inducted into the Baseball Hall of Fame.

The park was then an impressive facility. It had a press box wired for radio broadcasts, which was then a hot new technology. The first radio broadcast of a Buffs game occurred the previous season. The park was also equipped with lights by the 1930s, which allowed for night games to be played there. Anyone who has been out on a hot sunny Houston afternoon in July or August can appreciate how welcome night games were to Buffs fans. For the next three decades, Buffs Stadium was Houston's sports place. It was the site of the first night baseball game played between two major-league teams; the game was played on February 21, 1931, between the Chicago White Sox and New York Giants. The Houston Eagles, the city's

Finger's Furniture Warehouse Store was built on the site of Buffs Stadium. It hosted the Houston Sports Museum in the basement, which commemorated the location of Buffs Stadium's home plate with a replica on the spot. *Photograph by Brian Reading. Courtesy of www. commons.wikimedia.org.*

only Negro League team, also played at Buffs Stadium between 1949 and 1950. High school commencements and games also took place at Buffs Stadium. The University of Houston's Cougars baseball team played at Buffs Stadium in the 1940s. The stadium was just across US 75 from the campus, making it convenient to both the players and spectators.

Another, less desirable first also occurred in Buffs Stadium. In 1949, KLEE-TV began televising baseball games from Buffs Stadium, and on June 11, 1950, a man broke into the television booth of the press room at the stadium during the sixth inning of a game between the Buffs and the Tulsa Oilers. The man told Dick Gottlieb, who was broadcasting the game, "I got something to tell you." The man then sat down next to Gottlieb and the broadcast engineer, pulled out a revolver and shot himself. The cameras broadcast the noise of the shot and pictures of the man's slumped body. It was the nation's first televised suicide.

Buffs Stadium almost became home to the St. Louis Cardinals in 1952, when the team went up for sale and a group of Houston businessmen attempted to purchase it. Since the Buffs were also owned by the Cardinals, the Cardinals owned the major-league rights to Houston. This meant the Cardinals were able to move to Houston. Sadly, St. Louis–based Anheuser-Busch swept in and bought the Cardinals out from under the Houston consortium, keeping the team in St. Louis. Adding insult to injury, the new owners renamed Buffs Stadium Busch Stadium in 1957.

All good things must come to an end, and eventually, Buffs Stadium's reign as Houston's sports arena ended as well. By the late 1950s, the stadium was getting old. Even in 1952, it was too small to host a major-league team. (The attempt to move the Cardinals fell through in part because Buffs Stadium could not be brought up to the major league's standards.) Significant expansion of the stadium would be difficult, as the city had grown and enveloped the site. Houston was getting large enough to merit a major-league team, and it wanted a major-league team. The National and American Leagues were both expanding south and west from the Midwest and Atlantic Coast that had defined the major leagues between 1910 and 1950. A group of Houston investors were offering both leagues serious money to land an expansion franchise in Houston.

The Cardinals realized that minor-league ball could not compete with a major-league franchise, and they sold the Buffs after the 1958 season. The Buffs left the Texas League and moved into the Triple-A American Association minor league in 1959. The Buffs became an independent minor-league team in 1959, and in 1960, they joined the Chicago Cubs farm system. But the end was in sight for the Buffs; a group of Houston business leaders formed the Houston Sports Association, which worked with the City of Houston to win one of the eight new baseball franchises in a newly forming third major league: the Continental League. The Continental League disbanded before playing a game, so instead, the National and American Leagues agreed to expand and split the eight teams that had been planned for the Continental League between them.

One of the eight teams was a new major-league team for Houston. In 1962, Houston got its first major-league team—the Colt 45s, which became the Astros in 1965. The Buffs were purchased by the Houston Sports Association and were moved to Oklahoma City in 1962. As the Oklahoma City 89s, the team served as the Houston Colt 45s' and Astros' Triple-A farm team until 1972. The Colt 45s never played in Buffs Stadium; instead, they played in a temporary stadium called Colt Stadium during their 1962, 1963 and 1964 seasons. Interestingly, the stadium was located where today's NRG Stadium stands. In 1965, the Astros got a new stadium

Today, Finger's Furniture Warehouse is out of business. The warehouse is still there but is being used for commercial storage. *Photograph by author.*

along with their new name—the Astrodome, America's first enclosed major-league baseball stadium.

By then, Buffs Stadium was gone. With the departure of the Buffs and the pending arrival of the city's major-league team, the stadium became surplus to the needs of the town. There was a talk of preserving the stadium since it was part of Houston's heritage. It had been such an important part of the town's sports history. But in 1961, Hurricane Carla settled the issue. When the storm blew through Houston, it damaged Buffs Stadium seriously enough to make its restoration impractical. The old stadium was sold at auction for just $19,750 and was demolished in 1963. However, that was not the end of the old stadium. A Finger Furniture Center was erected at the site, and the store set up the Houston Sports Museum in its lower level. The centerpiece of the museum was a home plate that used by the Houston Buffs. Admission to the museum was free, and sports fans could view the exhibits while they were surrounded by Houston sports memorabilia.

Sadly, the Finger Furniture store closed in 2013. Fifty years after Buffs Stadium was demolished, Finger Furniture declared bankruptcy in January 2014. The Gulf Freeway property was sold later that year and the Houston Sports Museum closed permanently.

6.

THE DUTCHMAN AND JEFF DAVIS

The phrase "as cold as charity" came from the frequency with which charity, which is intended to be an act of unselfish kindness, is bestowed in a grudging way. For an example, consider the Jefferson Davis Hospital, Houston's charity hospital from the 1940s through 1980s. It was located at 1801 Buffalo (now Allen) Parkway and was the city's second central charity hospital. Houston was not big on indigent care back in the day but built its first charity hospital in 1924. To save money, the city put it up on city-owned land that had previously been used as a cemetery until the 1890s. The cemetery contained over 6,000 graves, and many of them contained nineteenth-century indigents that were buried at the city's expense. The dead also included several thousand Confederate soldiers who had died in Houston during the Civil War. To spare the expense of relocating the graves, the hospital's "basement" was built at ground level. To placate surviving Confederate veterans, the city named the hospital after Jefferson Davis, the former president of the Confederacy. The Jefferson Davis Hospital opened in 1925, in the midst of one of Houston's growth spurts. The four-story building soon proved to be inadequate, so a new facility was built at Buffalo Parkway.

This time, the city was determined to do it right, so they cleared away the blight of the Fourth Ward (which contained the homes of poor, black Houstonians). The new hospital, which was designed by noted architects Alfred Finn and Joseph Finger, was an eleven-story masterpiece of Style Moderne with five hundred beds. The building's cornerstone was laid in

1936, and the it was completed fifteen months later, in October 1937. The hospital had been known as the City-County Hospital until it opened, when it assumed the previous indigent hospital's name. (The old building became known for many years as Old Jefferson Davis Hospital.)

Despite the city's best efforts, the new charity hospital was soon bit by the same problem the first hospital faced: Houston's explosive growth. The hospital was adequate for a 1940 Houston population of 385,000, but Houston grew to have a population of 600,000 in 1950 and was home to over 1 million people by the 1960s. Many of these new residents used Jefferson Davis in the 1960s, and some even entered the city through the hospital. Between 1966 and 1989, over 286,000 babies were born in the hospital's delivery rooms. On occasion, the hospital would run out of cribs and would be forced to use temporary cardboard cribs instead. In one two-day period in July 1970, there were 64 births. Jefferson Davis was also the trauma center for the city's poor. Victims of car crashes, knife and gun fights, workplace

When the second Jefferson Davis Charity Hospital opened at 1801 Buffalo Parkway in 1937, it was an example of how a city government could do things right. It was large enough to accommodate its intended clients and was a handsome example of public architecture. *Photograph by Paul Hester.*

accidents and many other traumatic incidents poured into Jefferson Davis's emergency room. During flu season, sufferers crowded into the hospital's waiting room shoulder to shoulder. According to the *Houston Chronicle* in November 1960, the hospital saw a record 1,335 patients—in one day. The hospital's problems were exacerbated, because there was no one entity that was responsible for funding the hospital. Costs were shared between Harris County and the City of Houston, and each felt the other should have paid more. Neither would let the other take advantage of them; thus, despite the overcrowding, Jefferson Davis was chronically underfunded.

A new charity hospital, Ben Taub, was opened in South Houston in 1962. It was meant to ease Jefferson Davis's overcrowding, but it did not. Ben Taub was mostly used by the South-side poor who could not get to Jefferson Davis. The overcrowding situation slid from bad in the mid-1950s to incredibly worse by the mid-1960s. So, enter Jan de Hartog. De Hartog was born in Haarlem in the Netherlands in 1914, and he was the son of a theology professor father and university lecturer mother. He was not as scholarly as his parents, and at just eleven years old, he ran away to sea as a cabin boy. His father eventually brought him back, but he ran away again. He spent the next fifteen years knocking around on a number of Dutch ships. While de Hartog was not normally scholarly, some of his parents' abilities must have rubbed off. In his spare, time de Hartog wrote plays and pulp fiction stories that he often published under pseudonyms.

In 1939, he wrote a novel about Holland's deep-sea tug industry, which the Dutch considered Holland's glory. De Hartog even titled the novel *Holland's Glorie*. Set between 1890 and 1920, it was an apolitical novel that drew on de Hartog's seafaring experiences and stories that other Dutch sailors had told him. It was released in April 1940—just nine days before Germany invaded the Netherlands. The invasion turned *Holland's Glorie* into a bestseller, and it acted like a balm for the Netherlands' citizens after the humiliation of their defeat. The book became a metaphor for all that was great about the Netherlands. All of this turned de Hartog into a lightning rod for the Nazis. They were angered by anything that fostered resistance, even innocuous novels. After he was warned that he was about to be arrested by the Nazis, de Hartog went into hiding. In 1943, he crossed the English Channel and escaped to Britain. De Hartog served at sea for the rest of the war as a correspondent and a tugboat captain. Although he was a civilian, de Hartog's job was risky. Oceangoing tugboats assisted ships that had been damaged by U-boats, and they were frequently targets themselves.

By the 1960s, Jefferson Davis Hospital was grossly overcrowded and had inadequate resources for the patients using it. Even worse was that its funding was a part of a game of keep-away that was being played by the City of Houston and Harris County. *Photograph by Paul Hester.*

By 1945, de Hartog was the Netherlands' most famous living author. After the war, he began writing and publishing books in English as well as Dutch, and they all became bestsellers. He also remained in Britain, where he met and married his third (and final) wife, Marjorie. They bought a ninety-foot-long Dutch ship called the *Rival* and turned it into a houseboat before moving back to Holland. In 1957, the couple decided to move to the United States, and they brought the houseboat with them as deck cargo on a freighter. They had to land at a port with cranes large enough to hoist the *Rival* off the freighter. One of the few ports that could do this was Houston's, so that was where they went. After landing in Houston, the couple took the *Rival* up the Intercoastal Waterway to Nantucket, and de Hartog wrote a book about it.

Despite Houston's heat and humidity, the de Hartogs decided to return to the city. Maybe the city's flat, waterlogged terrain reminded them of the Netherlands. Or perhaps the heat and humidity reminded them of Batavia (called Jakarta today), a longtime Dutch colony. Or maybe it was University of Houston's invitation for Jan de Hartog to teach playwriting that convinced them to stay. (At the time, de Hartog had written several major plays, including *The Fourposter,* which became the musical *I Do! I Do!*) Whatever it was, the couple anchored the *Rival* in Brays Bayou and made Houston their home.

By then, de Hartog had also become a Quaker and a pacifist. Because of this, the de Hartogs regularly looked for volunteer work in the Houston area. At a party, Marjorie learned that there were too few nurses at Jefferson Davis Hospital to look after the babies and that volunteers were being sought to make up the difference. First, Marjorie volunteered, and then Jan volunteered to work as an orderly at Jefferson Davis. What Jan experienced there appalled him. One of his first encounters there was with a woman in a wheelchair who was hemorrhaging after being left with an untreated miscarriage. The woman was too weak to roll herself to registration, and she was being ignored by staff members, who were busy dealing with a flood of other patients. Blood and vomit covered the floors, the examination rooms were filthy, the tools were unsanitary and overcrowding was an everyday experience. The cages of the animals at the Houston Zoo were air conditioned, but the rooms at Jefferson Davis were not. The staff was not deliberately trying to make the patients at Jefferson Davis miserable; they did their best but lacked resources. There was too little of everything except patients; there were too few rooms and beds, too little equipment, too few doctors and nurses and even too few janitors.

For de Hartog, the breaking point came when he learned that the city council planned to cut the budget at Jefferson Davis Hospital. The city council felt that the money could be better spent elsewhere. Outraged, de Hartog wrote a letter protesting the decision, which was published in Houston's morning newspaper at the time, the *Houston Post*. It was ignored.

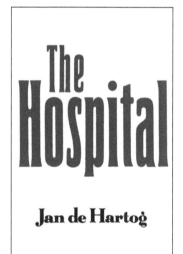

Jan de Hartog's book *The Hospital* provided a devastating exposé of conditions at Jefferson Davis Hospital. It ultimately led to badly needed reforms, although they came at highly personal cost to Jan and Marjorie de Hartog. *Photograph by author.*

De Hartog may have become a pacifist, but he remained a fighter. He used weapons that were appropriate for a best-selling author: words. He wrote a nonfiction exposé about his experiences as a volunteer at Jefferson Davis called *The Hospital*. Published in 1964, *The Hospital* recounted his experiences. It was blistering and exposed the horrible conditions that existed in the hospital—the overcrowding, the blood-spattered floors covered with cigarette butts, soiled bedding, a nurse removing a cockroach from a child's tracheotomy tube, patients hooked up to empty IV bags (because there was not enough staff to change or remove them)—it was all there.

The book's effects were explosive. Virtually every major weekly magazine in the United

States ran a cover story about the book and the state of the Jefferson Davis Hospital. Suddenly, Houston, which had advertised itself as the Space City in the 1960s, was exposed as the Third-World Medical System City. It was an unexpected—and undesired—form of attention. For reformers, the book became a rallying point. De Hartog led a fundraising drive that was intended to raise $60,000 to improve the conditions at Jefferson Davis and to ensure that Ben Taub was properly staffed. He put his money where his mouth was and donated $10,000 (the equivalent to nearly $80,000 today). He also donated his earnings from *The Hospital* to Houston's charity hospitals.

The de Hartogs and their allies also worked to establish a central taxing authority for Harris County's charity hospitals. The effort was aided by Houston's powerbrokers, who wanted to resolve the problem that was bringing embarrassing attention to the city. A referendum establishing the Harris County Hospital District, which was responsible for running the county's charity medical system, and a taxing authority to raise enough funds to run it was placed before Harris County voters in 1965. The referendum narrowly failed in the spring. It was again placed on the ballot in November, and that time, it passed. Starting on January 1, 1966, the Harris County Hospital District assumed responsibility for healthcare services in Harris County.

This victory came too late for Jan and Marjorie de Hartog, because by then, they were gone—they had left Houston the previous summer. His stand had created hostility and the two were shunned and became the subjects of abusive comments and anonymous threats. Once, they received a bag filled with excrement. The departure did not hurt de Hartog, and over the next twenty years, he released one best-selling book after another. His play *The Fourposter* was also transformed into the hit play *I Do! I Do!* In many ways, his wilderness years away from Houston proved to be the apex of his career as an author. However, Houston must have had a pull on the de Hartogs, because the couple quietly moved back to the city in the 1980s. They remained a beloved part of Houston's Quaker community until Jan de Hartog's death in September 2002.

The creation of the Harris County Hospital District transformed charity healthcare in Houston. The Ben Taub and Jefferson Davis hospitals did not become perfect (perfection is not possible), but they became much better places, and the abuses outlined in *The Hospital* were addressed. The Harris County Hospital District became the Harris Health System in 2012 and is now responsible for three hospitals and around thirty-six clinics that serve the poor and underinsured in Harris County. Ben Taub is now a level 1

The second Jefferson Davis Hospital was torn down in 1999. Other than a few architectural preservationists, no one objected. Today, the site is occupied by the Federal Reserve Bank of Dallas's Houston Branch Bank. *Photograph by William Lardas.*

trauma center—one of three in the Houston-Galveston Metropolitan Area. If you get into a car crash or a bad industrial accident in the Houston area, you will probably end up at Ben Taub.

Jefferson Davis Hospital is no longer a part of the Harris Health System. The Harris County Hospital District built a new hospital called the Lyndon B. Johnson Hospital in Northeast Houston in 1989. Shortly after, the Jefferson Davis Hospital was closed. The building stood largely vacant over the next decade before, finally, in 1999—despite the building's landmark status—it was torn down. Today, the Federal Reserve Bank of Dallas's Houston Branch Bank stands in that location, offering no clue to its former use as a hospital.

Jan de Hartog is no longer in Houston, either. After his death, he was cremated, and his ashes were scattered in the North Sea near the coast of the Netherlands—waters he knew and loved well. Ironically, the original Jefferson Davis Hospital still exists; the land it's located on cannot be sold due to the graveyard the hospital was built over. After years of neglect, it was declared a historical landmark and restored. Today, it is the Elder Street Artist Lofts. When people today talk about "Houston's Jefferson Davis" they think of that one—so thoroughly has de Hartog's hospital been forgotten.

7.

THE UNLUCKY SHAMROCK

The Shamrock Hotel was intended to be the grandest grand hotel in Texas—preferably in the entire Southern United States. Construction of the hotel started in 1946, the year after World War II ended, and was completed in 1949, just as the Cold War was heating up. Big, bold and brash—the Shamrock mirrored the attitude of late-1940s Houston. It was an era that promised no limit to Houston's growth, and unlimited growth was viewed as a good thing. The Shamrock seemed to be proof of that belief. It served as a Houston landmark for over thirty-eight years, from the 1940s to the 1980s.

The man behind the Shamrock was Glenn McCarthy, an independent Texas oilman. McCarthy was one of those larger-than-life figures that often appear in Texas. He grew up in the first half of the twentieth century and became involved in the oil industry rather than the cotton and cattle industries of the previous century. Author Edna Ferber used Glenn McCarthy as the model for Jett Rink, a character in her 1952 best-selling novel *Giant*. In the 1956 movie based on the novel, Rink was played by James Dean—a perfect reflection of the man who inspired the role. Born in 1907 in Beaumont, Texas, McCarthy grew up in a poor of Irish immigrants. He started working in the oilfields at age eight as a water boy, carrying water to drilling crews. After attending three universities on football scholarships, McCarthy dropped out and got married.

At twenty-four years old, McCarthy began to wildcat oil wells (explore for oil or gas in previously unproven and unexplored land). He became the

This photograph shows the Shamrock Hotel in a late stage of its construction. The Shamrock popped out of the prairie that was southwest of downtown Houston. It was Glenn McCarthy's dream to establish a world-class hotel in Houston. *Courtesy of the University of Houston Digital Archive Library.*

wildcatter's wildcatter during the Depression and earned the title the King of the Wildcatters. Between 1932 and 1942, he struck oil thirty-eight times on wildcat fields. By 1945, he had discovered 11 producing oilfields in Texas alone. By 1949, his net worth exceeded $200 million (over $2 billion today) and was fueled by royalties from 450 producing wells. By 1945, it seemed like everything he touched turned to gold, so he began to diversify his assets. Some business, such as the Houston Export Company, the McCarthy Chemical Company and the McCarthy International Tube Company, were at least related to his core oil business. But McCarthy also purchased newspapers, radio stations, a magazine, a movie production company and two banks—he even introduced McCarthy's Wildcatter Whiskey. McCarthy also bought a lot of land around Houston, including acreage around what later became the Astrodome and Sharpstown.

In 1946, Glenn McCarthy decided to go into the hotel business, and the result was the Shamrock Hotel. He plunged into the hotel scene on a Texas scale. The hotel was planned as a 1,100-room, eighteen-story building. It was the largest hotel built in the United States during the 1940s and contained an outdoor swimming pool that was 165 by 142 feet, which was, of course, the largest outdoor pool ever built at the time and was frequently advertised as being large enough to water ski on. Waterskiing exhibitions were repeatedly held at the pool. The hotel was flanked on one side by a five-story, one-thousand-car garage, which contained a 25,000-square-foot exhibition hall. On the other side was the pool, a terrace and a massive landscaped garden. The entire complex was housed on a 15-acre plot at the intersection of Main Street and Holcombe Boulevard. It was the first phase of what would become the McCarthy Center. When it was finished, a shopping center and entertainment complex joined the hotel.

While postwar Modernism was considered to be the latest trend in architecture in the late 1940s, McCarthy opted for a Style Moderne exterior for the Shamrock, a variant of Art Deco. By the 1940s, Style Moderne and Art Deco were considered old-fashioned, and the Shamrock would be the last major Style Moderne building erected in the United States. The hotel generated vinegary criticism by the nation's leading architects. Frank Lloyd Wright, upon visiting the Shamrock, commented, "I've often wondered what the inside of a jukebox looked like. Now I know." Wright later characterized the building as "architectural venereal disease."

The hotel's interior was opulent. It was filled with marble, Bolivian mahogany paneling and elaborate furnishings. Every room had air conditioning, a television, push button radios and art. One-third of the rooms also had kitchenettes. Today, televisions and air conditioning are expected—even in low-budget hotels—but in the 1940s, they were extraordinary amenities. Most Houston homes lacked air conditioning, and in 1949, Houston had just one television station. The Shamrock also had an Irish theme—a nod to McCarthy's Irish heritage. Its ashtrays, dishes,

The cover of a brochure touting the Shamrock's amenities. The hotel had several clubs and restaurants, a tennis court and a swimming pool large enough to water-ski on. *Courtesy of the University of Houston Digital Archive Library.*

wastebaskets and walls were emblazoned with Shamrocks, and no fewer than sixty-three different shades of green were used in interior decoration. (No one could accuse the Shamrock of being a two-bit hotel. It obviously used a six-bit registry.)

The Shamrock's most audacious feature was its location. The Holcombe and Main intersection, which is within today's Interstate 610 Loop, is considered deep within Houston's downtown area in the twenty-first century. In 1946, when the ground was broken for the hotel, the interstate system was still a decade in the future. The corner of Holcombe and Main was, at the time, a long three miles from central downtown. The area was a suburb at the time—and a low-density suburb at that. McCarthy was putting a downtown-sized hotel on Houston's edge, amid a coastal prairie. Although there were plans to put the Texas Medical Center next to the Shamrock, no one believed that it would be able to pull downtown levels of traffic to the luxury hotel. Hospitals were for sick people—and local ones at that. Most Houston powerbrokers thought McCarthy was crazy. McCarthy countered that he was crazy like a fox. He believed that Houston would decentralize due to the growing popularity of the automobile. The city's growth was moving south and west. In the late 1940s, there were plans to construct a freeway past the Shamrock.

McCarthy sank $22 million of his $200 million fortune into building the Shamrock. When construction was completed, the Shamrock was the largest and most luxurious hotel in Texas and the largest hotel in the United States outside of Los Angeles and New York. Critics may have hated the Shamrock's architecture and furnishings but Houstonians loved it. McCarthy's over-the-top approach fit perfectly with the boisterous energy of 1950s and 1960s Houston. Everything seemed larger in Houston; there were fortunes to be made for those who worked hard, and the city was shooting for the moon (quite literally after NASA moved there). Just as Edna Ferber modeled Jett Rink on Glenn McCarthy, she put the Shamrock in *Giant* and transformed it into the Conquistator. The hotel opened in 1949—on St. Patrick's Day, of course.

The hotel's grand opening was Texas-sized; McCarthy invited 175 Hollywood entertainers and film executives to the opening bash. One planeload arrived on a Boeing 307 Stratoliner that McCarthy had purchased from Howard Hughes just a few days earlier. Others came by rail from Los Angeles on a chartered Santa Fe Super Chief. Pat O'Brian, Ginger Rogers, Errol Flynn and Lana Turner attended. Dorothy Lamour, the World War II pinup girl, kicked off the first performance at the Shamrock. Journalists from across the country were also invited. The celebration even included a parade and an estimated forty-two-dollar-per-plate grand opening dinner that was attended by 2,000 paying guests. An estimated 50,000 members of the public also came to gawk at Houston's newest grand hotel. The party turned rowdy and raucous as Houstonians boisterously celebrated the new landmark. Things got so lively that a nationwide radio broadcast that had been scheduled for the evening had to be canceled. The intended host, Dorothy Lamour, reportedly abandoned ship, fleeing the stage in tears.

After the Shamrock's grand opening, the hotel became a focus of Houston's social scene. Between 1949 and 1953, the hotel hosted "Saturday at the Shamrock," a nationally broadcast radio show produced by the American Broadcasting Corporation. It was the only scripted nationally broadcast radio show produced outside of Los Angeles and New York. In 1959, Maxine Messinger, *Houston Press*'s gossip columnist, moved into the Shamrock with her seven-year-old son. Soon thereafter, she began broadcasting a local radio show on Houston's social scene from the hotel. It stayed on the air through her move to the *Houston Chronicle* and well into the 1980s.

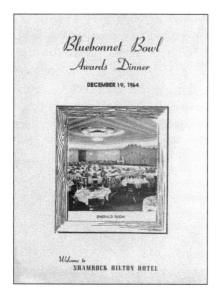

The Shamrock often hosted important events, including sports award dinners. This is the program for the 1964 Bluebonnet Bowl Dinner. The Bluebonnet Bowl was held annually in Houston between 1959 and 1987. *Courtesy of the University of Houston Digital Archive Library.*

The Shamrock was also a magnet for celebrities—both national and local; the rich and famous partied there. College football teams that were participating in Houston's Bluebonnet Bowl often stayed at the Shamrock. The Emerald Room, a nightclub, and Cork Club, a private social club, were located at the Shamrock. Both became legendary—the Emerald Room for the entertainers it showcased, and the Cork Club for the oil deals that were consummated there. The Shamrock soon became known as the "Houston Riviera."

While the Shamrock was known for attracting famous guests, it was also popular with ordinary Houstonians. The hotel was the scene of the annual Easter egg hunt and (of course) St. Patrick's Day parade. It was also the place where Houstonians held their proms, weddings, bar mitzvahs and school reunions. Sports clubs that were organized by the hotel gave Houstonians access to the pool and tennis courts for a nominal fee. Locals flocked to the place. Despite this success, the critics were proven to have been right about the Shamrock's location. U.S. 59 was ultimately rerouted west of Main Street after the hotel was completed, reducing the amount of traffic that McCarthy had planned on when he built the place. The location was proved to be too far from Houston's central downtown to attract 1950s business travelers, and maintaining occupancy became a problem.

McCarthy lost control of the Shamrock in 1953 but not because it was losing money. When McCarthy owned the Shamrock, it remained profitable, but it was a reliable producer instead of the gusher that McCarthy had counted on. McCarthy's business empire had been overextended and eventually collapsed. While the Shamrock turned a profit, his newspapers and movie studio bled money. Some of his oil plays also failed to deliver, and his land investments went sour. By 1952, McCarthy was $52 million in debt. When he defaulted on his loans, the Equitable Life Assurance Company took control of the Shamrock. McCarthy maintained a right of redemption on the hotel but was no longer running it. McCarthy eventually recovered, and the federal government gave him an unprecedented private loan to cover his debt. He cleared much of that debt by selling his land holdings and unprofitable businesses. However, the fun left the Shamrock when he was no longer managing it. He sold his right of redemption to Hilton Hotels in 1954. From then on, the hotel was known as the Shamrock-Hilton. The corporation ran the place on a much less opulent scale than McCarthy had. The Cork Club departed the hotel, and McCarthy reopened in it a skyscraper in downtown Houston in 1957. Although the Shamrock-Hilton remained a focus of the Houston social scene for many years, it was never quite the same.

The Hilton chain ran the Shamrock for the next thirty years, but the hotel's location eventually led to its demise. It was a hotel made for conventions that was located too far from downtown to be convenient for them. It was built on too big a scale, and Hilton always had trouble filling its 1,100 rooms. This problem only grew worse over time. The Galleria, with its shopping center, hotels and convention center, opened in 1970 and was a fulfillment of McCarthy's original dream for the Shamrock. Located off Interstate 610 on Houston's west side, the Galleria was easier to get to than the Shamrock and was newer, glitzier and more glamorous. The Galleria also drew traffic away from the Shamrock-Hilton; its cheaper and more car-friendly motels

Today, only the Shamrock's parking structure still exists. On the site of the hotel, a new building was erected that now houses Texas A&M's Institute of Biosciences and Technology department. *Photograph by author.*

grew more popular in the 1960s and 1970s, siphoning away more business. As the 1970s became the 1980s, it became increasingly difficult for Hilton to keep occupancy rates high enough to keep the old hotel profitable.

The hotel itself had also grown old, and what had been new and appealing in 1950 was old-fashioned and frumpy by 1980. Restoring the Shamrock to 1980's standards of a luxury hotel required an expensive makeover. Houston was experiencing one of its periodic oil busts in 1985, and this one was quite severe. Hilton decided that renovating the hotel would just be a waste of good money. That year, Hilton threw in the towel and sold the Shamrock to the Texas Medical Center at a giveaway price. The Texas Medical Center had no need for a luxury hotel, so it decided to tear it down. Historical preservationists protested the destruction of the hotel and held a massive rally at the Shamrock on St. Patrick's Day in 1986. One attendee was Glenn McCarthy, who was by then living in quiet retirement in a modest two-story frame house in La Porte, a Houston suburb. Their protests were ignored, and the demolition of the Shamrock proceeded. Wreckers started tearing down the building on June 1, 1987, and demolition was complete by September. McCarthy's kidneys failed a year later, and he died on December 26, 1988.

Today, the site of the Shamrock is home to Texas A&M's Institute of Biosciences and Technology, a part of the Texas A&M campus at the Texas Medical Center. Only the Shamrock's parking structure remains. The Medical Center kept that, because there is always a need for parking in Houston.

8.

PBS'S FIRST STAND

E verybody knows that watching television is "bad for you." Yet, few things dominated the last half of the twentieth century as much as television. The first major growth of television stations in the United States occurred in 1948, and by 1960—a bare dozen years later—it was an essential part of the American experience. People planned their lives around the television schedule. There were only a dozen VHF stations (viewers with a box on their set could also pick up weird snow-filled UHF stations), and normally, viewers were lucky if they could even pick up just half of those channels. But were people using television to better themselves? No. Comedies like *I Love Lucy*, *Leave It to Beaver* and *Father Knows Best*; westerns like *Gunsmoke* and *Have Gun Will Travel*; and dramas like *Perry Mason* and *77 Sunset Strip* filled weeknights. There were science fiction shows like *The Twilight Zone* and quiz shows like *What's My Line*. Sunday evenings were filled with the *Ed Sullivan Show* and Saturday mornings were packed with a glorious (if you were a kid) array of cartoons. Television was the boob tube. Federal Communications Commission (FCC) chairman Newton N. Minow called commercial television "a vast wasteland" in a speech he gave at the National Association of Broadcasters on May 9, 1961. Parents chased their kids away from television sets and out to the backyard to play—and then the parents settled before the TV and spent the rest of the day there.

However, there was one oasis in that vast wasteland: public television. Kids that grew up in the 1960s and 1970s knew that watching public television was supposed to be good for you. It was *educational*—a word that excused much. The benefits of watching public television instead of commercial networks can be debated. What cannot be debated (and what had the cultural elites of New York and Los Angeles green with envy) was that the first public television station to go on the air was located in Houston, Texas. The channel was called KUHT-TV, Houston's channel 8.

The first television station in the United States, an experimental station run by GE out of Schenectady, New York, began broadcasting in 1928. Growth was slow in those early years, and it was not until 1941 that the FCC felt that television was mature enough for commercial licensing. Ten stations were licensed by December 1941, and most of them were located in New York and Los Angeles, with the exception of one that was located in Philadelphia. America's abrupt entry into World War II on December 7, 1941, put a freeze on television's growth for the next four years. Four of the ten stations suspended broadcasting until the war's end, and the rest cut back their broadcasting hours. Television production for civilian use ceased until August 1945, limiting audience growth. However, once the war ended and restrictions were lifted, television grew explosively. During World War II, companies could apply for a broadcast permit even if they could not build a station. Permitting was simple: fill out a short form, mail it to the FCC and wait for the reply—which was virtually automatic.

This system worked at first because there were more available licenses than requests, but that quickly reversed. Permit requests began flooding in. Just in Texas, there were twenty-five applications or permits on file by August 1948. The FCC realized that its first-come-first-serve process was not working. To allow time to study the issue, the FCC froze applications for VHF broadcast licenses on September 30, 1948. Only stations that were already broadcasting or under construction were allowed to keep their broadcast licenses. This policy left Texas with six stations. WBAP on channel 5 in Fort Worth began broadcasting on September 29. It was soon joined by KLRD-TV on channel 4 and KBTV-TV on channel 8 in Dallas; KEYL-TV on channel 5 and WOAI-TV on channel 4 in San Antonio and KLEE-TVon channel 2 in Houston. (KLRD is today's KDFW; KBTV is now WFAA; KEYL is KENS and KLEE has become KPRC.) These six stations remained Texas's only broadcast stations for the next four years.

When deciding how to allocate channels, the FCC would consider color stations and the role that educational television should play. The study went on for years; after all, no federal bureaucrat feels time pressure. A wrong decision could cause *criticism*, so it's better to ponder a little longer. It was not until April 14, 1952, that the FCC resumed issuing permits. One effect of

The sign-on logo for KUHT-TV. Houston's channel 8 was the first public interest television station to begin broadcasting in the United States. The original studio was in the Ezekial Cullen Building, which is in the background of this picture. *Courtesy of the University of Houston Digital Archive Library.*

the FCC's four-year freeze was part of the television spectrum was allocated for public interest broadcasting. Nationwide, 242 channels were set aside for noncommercial educational purposes; of those, 80 were in the mainstream VHF band. The other 162 were allocated in the then-experimental UHF frequencies. In cities like Los Angeles, New York and Washington, D.C.— early adapters of television—the VHF spectrum was already pretty full, so the educational channels were assigned to UHF channels. In Texas, Houston, Dallas and San Antonio each bagged one of the 80 public interest VHF channels. The FCC granted 5 additional channels to Houston in 1952—channels 8, 13, 23, 29 and 32—and Galveston got channel 11. With the inclusion of channel 2, which became KPRC-TV after the *Houston Post* bought KLEE-TV in 1950, the Houston-Galveston metropolitan area had seven television stations—four in VHF. Channel 8 was reserved for noncommercial educational purposes.

The University of Houston had an active communications department and already offered courses in radio communications. It launched the first university-operated broadcast radio station in November 1950, so television

This image shows the interior of KUHT-TV's broadcasting studio. In the station's early days, most of KUHT-TV's workers were students who were learning skills that they hoped to use after college. *Courtesy of the University of Houston Digital Archive Library.*

was the obvious next step. The university, upon receiving internal approval, applied for a television broadcast license on April 17, 1951. When the FCC's freeze was lifted in 1952, the University of Houston was the only applicant for Houston's noncommercial channel. The license for channel 8 was soon granted to the University of Houston.

The president of University of Houston, Walter W. Kemmerer, viewed television as a unique way to cut education costs while expanding course offerings. He estimated that using a television to broadcast classes the University of Houston could save $10 million in construction costs by reducing need for lecture halls. The problem was that setting up a station was expensive. To become a functioning station after receiving a license would have cost the university $250,000, the equivalent to about $2.5 million today. This was a problem faced by every potential public station in 1952 in Los Angeles and New York, as well as Houston. However, Houston had an angel to help it though: oil baron Hugh Roy Cullen.

Cullen, who was born in 1881, grew up in poverty in San Antonio, Texas. In 1915, after an early career as a cotton buyer, he abandoned cotton for the risky—but high-payoff—oil industry. After several years of buying leases in Central and West Texas, and after drilling nothing but dry holes, Cullen began to focus his wildcatting in the Houston area. Cullen's wife complained that he was spending too much time away from home, so they moved the family to Houston. When he arrived, he struck oil on the first try. The strike led to the development of a multimillion-dollar oil company.

One problem with becoming fabulously wealthy through oil is making money faster than it can be spent. By the time he turned fifty, Cullen, with his wife's support, decided to unload some of his surplus wealth through philanthropy. Perhaps due to his own blighted educational opportunities, he decided to help Texas colleges. In 1938, the couple donated $335,000 to build the University of Houston's first permanent building. Cullen continued contributing to the University of Houston, and in 1946, he donated the land that became Texas Southern University (Houston's historically black college and university). He set up the Cullen Foundation, a charity supporting education and medicine in 1954. By the time of his death in 1957, Cullen left behind 90 percent of his personal fortune. Cullen was enthusiastic about supporting the University of Houston's television station, and the Ford Foundation was offering a $1 match for every locally raised $2, up to $150,000. Cullen contributed most of the $165,000 raised in Houston. The Ford Foundation match provided the rest.

With a license and funding, Kemmerer moved ahead with getting the station on the air. He named Dr. John C. Schwarzwalder, a professor in the university's Radio-Television Department, the station's general manager. The school quickly set up a studio on the fifth floor of the Ezekiel Cullen Building (another building funded by Hugh Roy Cullen); the studio had been used by the university's radio station but was repurposed for television. Students were recruited to staff the station; art students created sets, communications students operated cameras, music students performed music and journalism students prepared scripts. Employing students cut operating costs, while giving the students college credit and practical experience. The station, KUHT-TV, went live on May 25, 1953; it was the eleventh television station to start broadcasting in Texas and was the first noncommercial television station in the United States. It beat out the next public interest station to air, Los Angeles's KTHE on channel 28 by six months. (KTHE was also funded by oil money but went off the air

KUHT-TV's first transmission antenna was mounted atop an oil rig that was donated to the University of Houston by Hugh Roy Cullen. It had previously been used for the University of Houston's radio station. *Courtesy of the University of Houston Digital Archive Library.*

in September 1954. It did not resume broadcasting until 1964. KUHT has broadcast continuously since May 1953.) New York would not get public television until the 1960s.

Two hours and thirty-three minutes of broadcasting followed the station's first sign-on at 5:00 p.m. on May 25. The lineup included *It's Five* (starting at 5:00 p.m.), *Bookland* (a fifteen-minute newscast), *Open House* (best described as an academic variety show) and *Experiment in Teaching*. The transmitter was located atop an oil derrick on campus, which was donated to serve as a broadcast tower by none other than Hugh Roy Cullen. While KUHT-TV regularly broadcast news, public interest shows and occasional movies, the station's emphasis during its early years was education. Nearly 40 percent of its air time went to broadcasting classes. KUHT televised forty different college courses during its early years. The first to be aired was Psychology 231, and English, beginning biology, chemistry, foreign language and even "Electricity in the Home" courses came afterward. Most classes were broadcast at night, so working people could take them.

Going live drew national attention. NBC's *Today Show*, which was then just one year old, filmed a four-and-a-half-minute feature, complete with an introduction by host Dave Garroway welcoming KUHT to the air. It did not take long for the national media to begin criticizing the station. The *New York Times* ran an article in March 1954 predicting an early demise for KUHT-TV. Yet channel 8 was already a popular spot for Houston television viewers. Three-quarters of the 200,000 sets that were estimated to be in the channel's broadcast area tuned into channel 8 at least once a week. The number is even more remarkable since KUHT-TV only broadcast Monday through Friday and was only on the air for twenty-eight hours per week. It gained popularity through its community service programing, which included broadcasting the Houston Independent School Board meetings that were projected to a live studio audience. Their reactions—cheers and boos—enlivened the broadcast.

The Ezekial Cullen Building served as KUHT's studios until 1964, when the broadcast studios moved to the Texas Television Center on Cullen Boulevard. The Texas Television Center had been home to the defunct

This image shows the Ezekiel Cullen building as it appears today. It is largely used as an administration building. Mature trees hide much of its lower floors. *Photograph by author.*

DuMont Television Network affiliate KNUZ-TV from 1953 to 1954 before it was purchased by KTRK-TV. It then served as KTRK-TV's studios from 1954 to 1961. In 1961, KHOU-TV also relocated its transmitter site and donated it and its antenna in Alvin to KUHT. This gave KUHT access to an eighty-mile transmission radius from Alvin, and by then, KUHT-TV was part of the Public Broadcasting System (PBS). It abandoned broadcasting classes in 1959, largely due to legislation banning the funding of broadcast classes, but PBS and Gulf Region Educational Television Associates (GRETA) gave it more than enough programing.

Today, the channel broadcasts from a tower in Missouri City, which has a one-hundred-mile reach. Its broadcast studio is back on the University of Houston's main campus, which is now known as the Cullen Campus. It has been in the state-of-the-art LeRoy and Lucile Melcher Center for Public Broadcasting since 2000. The Ezekiel Cullen Building, where the channel aired the first broadcast of public television in the nation, is now the University of Houston's administration building. The original studio is now a suite of administrative offices. It is not marked, so visitors must ask to be shown to the location.

9.

BOX IT

On May 1, 1956, a ship that was five days out from Newark, New Jersey, entered the Port of Houston to unload cargo. The ship was tied up at the Long Reach wharves on the south side of Buffalo Bayou, just downstream of the Turning Basin. The ship, which had been christened the SS *Ideal-X* months earlier, had begun life as a tanker called the SS *Potrero Hills* in 1944. It was one of over five hundred T-2 tankers that were built between 1942 and 1945. These mass-produced ships were built to meet the navy's emergency need for fuel-carrying ships during World War II. They could carry anything from aviation gasoline to crude oil. At the end of the war, the demand for tankers dropped, and many, including *Potrero Hills*, had been laid up as surplus or sold at a discount to commercial shipping companies.

Ideal-X was not being used as a tanker; instead, it carried dry goods. A record of the goods carried is forgotten today, but it was probably a collection of mixed nonperishable goods—machine parts, raw materials for Texas factories and consumer goods—things that are now normally carried aboard long-haul trucks. However, the cargo that was unloaded on that particular day was the most important cargo ever unloaded at the Port of Houston—more important than the cargo unloaded by *Laura* in January 1837. It was more important than the first oceangoing cargo unloaded by the SS *Morgan* in April 1876 or the cargo delivered by SS *Satilla* in August 1915, the first cargo ship to unload a cargo at Houston after the completion of the Houston Ship Channel. The *Ideal-X*'s cargo changed Houston and the world.

This image shows the *Ideal-X* after unloading cargo. A former tanker, the ship was converted to carry shipping containers. It carried the first commercial load of shipping containers and unloaded them at the Port of Houston. *Courtesy of the Port of Houston Authority.*

It was not what *Ideal-X* carried that changed everything but how the goods were packaged. They were carried in metal boxes designed to fit a standard forty-foot-long flatbed trailer, the kind that are common on the nation's highways today. The *Ideal-X* carried fifty-eight containers stacked two-high on its deck. The containers were lifted off *Ideal-X*'s deck and onto the flatbed trailers of fifty-eight waiting semi-trucks. The tractor-trailer rigs drove off once the containers were secured to the flatbed trailers. The unloading of the *Ideal-X* was completed in hours and was the first successful use of shipping containers.

Shipping containers changed everything; they created today's global economy. They also destroyed many of the twentieth century's largest seaports, while they turned minor ports into powerhouses of international commerce. They changed the way cargoes were handled, how ships were built and where industries were located. Without shipping containers, the world would be a much different—and poorer—place than it is today. And the container revolution started in Houston, Texas.

Malcom McLean was not trying to change the world when he invented the shipping container; he was simply trying to improve his bottom line and squeeze a little more profit out of his businesses. Malcolm McLean was a trucker, and he started his company in 1934 with a single-used truck. In the 1950s, he owned one of the largest trucking companies in the United States, which employed some 1,800 rigs. Trucking was labor-intensive, not just for drivers but for those who were loading and unloading the trucks as well. Cargo-handling at ports was expensive, too. With the exception of bulk cargoes—liquids such as petroleum products, grain and ore—everything had to be loaded onto pallets, and the pallets had to be loaded into the ship. At that point, armies of longshoremen and stevedores had to pack the cargoes into the ship—by hand. When the ship arrived at its destination, the process reversed itself; cargoes were placed on pallets, winched out of the hold onto the dock and loaded onto boxcars, flatcars and truck trailers. These goods were called break-bulk cargo, and it made up most of the world's freight in 1956, as it had since oceangoing ships had begun transporting goods.

Before the introduction of shipping containers, it could take a week to unload a ship after it arrived and another week to reload it for its next destination. In the meantime, the ship would just sit in harbor, not moving goods. A ship only earned money when it was at sea. It was also common for goods to be damaged in the process of loading and unloading or to disappear as longshoremen supplemented their income by appropriating small high-value goods. For example, a crate of alcohol would be "accidentally" dropped, the contents would be reported broken—a few bottles may have been broken to provide verisimilitude to the story—but the volume of whiskey spilled was much less than the contents of the crate. Or a bale containing watches would "split open" during unloading, a report would be filed that said the watches had been spilled into the water between the hull and wharf, but no one would send a diver to salvage the waterlogged watches, which were likely not there to find.

McLean wanted to load the content of his trucks onto ships without unloading them at departure and reloading upon arrival. At first, he tinkered with the idea of lifting the trucks' trailers onto the ships' decks. This was an old concept, as ships had been ferrying railroad cars since the end of the nineteenth century. Moving trailers by sea from one U.S. port to another also eliminated highway taxes that were incurred by driving the trailers cross-country. However, this idea proved uneconomical; the wheels and chassis took up too much space. Then, McLean hit on the concept of just loading the van portion of the trailer aboard the ship. He also discovered that strengthening the containers would allow them to be stacked, increasing cargo capacity significantly. In January 1956, he and his partners bought

Before the containerization of cargo, goods were shipped as break-bulk cargo and carried on pallets or in sacks. Loading and unloading these pallets was labor intensive and time consuming and could keep a ship in port for weeks. *Courtesy of the University of Houston Digital Archive Library.*

two T-2 tankers and converted them to be able to carry deck cargo, and he found customers who were willing to ship their goods via containers. The main difficulty he encountered was finding ports that were willing to handle containers. The longshore unions were strongly opposed to the concept and refused to handle them at the terminals they controlled. Newark had a nonunion terminal and so did Houston at its Long Reach terminal. So, the *Ideal-X* sailed from Newark to Houston.

The experiment was a success. The *Ideal-X* had no return cargo when it left Newark, but it was fully booked for a return trip by the time it arrived in Houston—McLean was in the container business. Within a year, McLean converted a new ship to carry containers; the SS *Gateway City* was another wartime build. It started life as SS *Iberville* and was drafted into the U.S. Navy as the fast attack transport *Sumter*, which carried troops in the Pacific. When the ship was decommissioned in 1946, it sat idle until McLean purchased it and converted it to carry 226 containers, which was nearly four times *Ideal-X*'s capacity.

Soon, McLean sold his trucking company (to avoid anti-trust issues) and was in the container shipping business full time. His company was named SeaLand and became one of the largest shipping companies in the world. While it started with a circuit covering U.S. ports in New Jersey, Florida, Puerto Rico and Texas, it grew to cover ports throughout the world. What made shipping containers so powerful were the savings they yielded. They cut the cost of cargo handling from $5.86 per ton to $0.16 per ton. That alone cut shipping costs by 97 percent, but that was just the beginning. A container ship carrying five thousand tons of cargo could be loaded and unloaded in a day, while a break-bulk cargo ship required two to three weeks to unload and load. A container ship spent 80 to 90 percent less time in port—time it used instead to ship cargoes.

No one initially realized the full implications of these cost reductions, including Malcom McLean. At first, the containers were just thought of as a seagoing version of air mail or a fast way to send express, high-value cargoes. The speed and convenience of containerized shipping was key, and it was the focus of early containerization. But not everyone needed to move their freight quickly, so the industry's initial growth was slow. Containers required specialized equipment to load and unload the containers, limiting the ports that could handle them.

It was not until the mid-1960s that containerization really took off. At the time, the United States was mired in a war in Vietnam, and the military needed to ship large quantities of supplies—containers were just what the logisticians ordered. In 1966, the U.S. government signed a contract with SeaLand to transport supplies across the Pacific. Through the 1970s, however, naval architecture professors still believed containers to be a passing fad. The first oil embargo in 1973 raised fuel prices dramatically, making the thirty-knot container ships uneconomical. Then, suddenly, everyone seemed to realize that cost, not speed, was the critical factor in shipping. Because container ships cut cargo handling costs by up to 95 percent, it really did not matter whether container ships went thirty knots or ten knots, they were still a lot more profitable than break-bulk ships. Those savings accrued whether the ships were carrying expensive electronics or cheap shirts. Suddenly, break-bulk goods with low profit margins were profitable cargoes when shipped by container. By virtually eliminating transportation costs, shipping containers created the global economy. Raw materials for labor-intensive goods could be shipped to low-wage countries, where they were finished and shipped to customers for less than it cost to have those goods manufactured in high-wage countries.

This image shows the Barbour's Cut Container Terminal. The Port of Houston remains a major leader in containerization, and its two newest container terminals account for over 50 percent of the cargo handled by the port. *Courtesy of the Port of Houston Authority.*

Whole industries moved from one country to another. The price of consumer goods dropped, and international trade skyrocketed.

The container revolution also changed the geography of shipping. Becoming a container port required significant capital investment; loading and unloading facilities, cranes to hoist containers off and on ships and roads and railroads for trucks and railcars to offload and receive containers from ships had to be purchased and built. Ports also had to scrap their existing infrastructure, because wharves designed around break-bulk cargoes were inefficient when dealing with containers. Some of the world's busiest ports, especially those with strong longshoremen's unions, ignored the containers and waited for the fad to pass. These included London, Liverpool, New York and New Orleans. These ports clung to traditional cargo handing until it was too late, because new ports, hungry for traffic, had already built container-handling facilities.

Felixstowe, a minor port in 1920, became Britain's largest port a century later by embracing containerization. London and Liverpool slipped to obscurity. New Orleans, the Gulf Coast's largest seaport in 1920, was eclipsed by the upstart Port of South Louisiana, thirty-three miles upriver from the Port of New Orleans. The Port of South Louisiana stretches for fifty-four miles along the length of the Mississippi River between New Orleans and Baton Rouge, and it built state-of-the-art container facilities in the late twentieth century. It is now the largest port in the United States, with twice the shipping tonnage of any other American port—with the exception of Houston—and nearly three times the tonnage of New Orleans.

The Port of Houston was one of the world's first two container ports. It remained a leader in container technology and was the port to which the world came to learn how to ship containers. Houston installed container cranes in the turning basin as the 1950s ended. It opened Barbours Cut, Texas's first cargo container terminal, in 1977, which was followed by

Ideal-X unloaded its first batch of containers at Long Reach Docks. This image shows Long Reach as it appears today. It is scheduled for a major renovation. *Courtesy of the Port of Houston Authority.*

the massive, seven-container-berth Bayport Terminal in 2006. Today, the Port of Houston handles over 2 million tons of cargo annually, with nearly 60 percent of that being container cargo. The gangs of longshoremen have been replaced by crane operators, cargo handlers and a slew of skilled laborers working for high wages; 1.35 million jobs are directly or indirectly attributable to the Port of Houston. The port is six times larger than it was in 1956.

SeaLand sold *Ideal-X* in 1959 and renamed it was renamed the *Elemir*. In February 1964, it was damaged in a storm and scrapped in Japan later that year. The Long Reach docks are still in use today and are now owned by the Port of Houston. The cotton sheds behind the wharf, where *Ideal-X* was tied up over fifty years earlier with its historic cargo, are being rebuilt as part of a general port upgrade. The wharf, where *Ideal-X* docked, has no marker to commemorate the event, but perhaps that does not matter. Due to the increased security following the 9/11 attack, the public is not permitted into the working areas of the Port of Houston. To reach the spot, visitors need a Transportation Worker Identification Credential (TWIC) card.

10.

BEFORE HOUSTON
BECAME SPACE CITY

Houston is Space City; its image is inextricably entangled with space exploration, especially manned spaceflight. The first word broadcast from a planetary surface other than Earth, was "Houston," spoken by Neil Armstrong from the moon's surface. In all, Armstrong said, "Houston, the Eagle has landed," proclaiming our conquest of space. Today, more than fifty years after Armstrong uttered those words, space remains big in Houston. All NASA manned space programs are run out of Johnson Space Center (JSC). JSC employs over seventeen thousand people—three thousand civil servants and fourteen thousand contractors. Ellington Field, a longtime partner of JSC, is adding commercial spaceport facilities for the new, privately owned manned spacecraft companies. One of Houston's biggest tourist attractions is Space Center Houston, Johnson Space Center's visitor's center, and it draws over one million visitors, annually. The city gives major league sports teams space-themed names: Aeros, Astros and Rockets.

However, Houston's space heritage is relatively new. The Manned Spacecraft Center (MSC), today's Johnson Space Center, was opened in Houston in late 1961, which was almost exactly seven years before Apollo 8 circled the moon to broadcast their famous reading of Genesis on Christmas Eve and less than eight years before Armstrong spoke to Houston from the Moon. For the first three years the center was in Houston, it was not managed from the towering Building 1 Headquarters Building that currently dominates JSC. Instead, its headquarters was located in an obscure building that now houses the City of Houston's Parks and Recreation Department.

NASA rented the Farnsworth & Chambers Building in Southeast Houston to use as their temporary headquarters building. This image shows the building as it appeared shortly after it was occupied by NASA. *Courtesy of the National Aerospace and Space Administration (NASA).*

When the Mercury Program was announced in 1958, it was assigned to the newly formed National Aeronautics and Space Administration (NASA) as their first manned project. NASA created the Space Task Group to oversee Project Mercury. It was based at Langley Research Center in Hampton Virginia, the oldest—and at the time, the largest—NASA field center. Following the 1960 election of President John F. Kennedy, a greater emphasis was placed on human spaceflight, so the Space Task Group became the Manned Spacecraft Center. NASA's director, James Webb, decided that the MSC needed its own facility independent of Langley. In August 1961, Webb appointed a committee to select the site for the new field center. On September 19, 1961, the committee reported its recommendation: Houston, Texas.

Everyone had expected the center to move to Texas—Kennedy's vice president, Lyndon Johnson had pretty much demanded a piece of the space program, as he was a space enthusiast and wanted his home state of Texas to get into the action—but why Houston? El Paso was already the gateway to the White Sands missile range. The committee had set four criteria for the Manned Spacecraft Center: it had to be near a major metropolitan center to ensure a skilled workforce was available; it had to be near a military airbase to provide air access that could be controlled by NASA; it had to be near a major research college to provide support for the expected scientific research delivered by space exploration, and finally, it needed to be near a port. No one really knew what a manned spacecraft center was supposed to do, but they thought it might involve testing big booster rockets, which could only be moved by water.

In 1961, most of the other potential sites in Texas met some but not all of these requirements. Victoria only had an airfield, El Paso lacked a port and a research college, Corpus Christi lacked a research college and Austin lacked a port. Houston, however, met all four requirements: it had a major seaport, a population of nearly one million people (including many technical workers), Ellington Air Force Base and Rice University (upgraded from its old title of Rice Institute in 1959), a respected research university.

The Mercury 7 astronauts pose for a publicity photograph behind the sign for the Manned Spacecraft Center's headquarters at the Farnsworth & Chambers Building in 1962 or 1963. *Courtesy of the National Aerospace and Space Administration (NASA).*

Additionally, Rice came with a bonus. Humble Oil had over one thousand acres of undeveloped pastureland adjoining Clear Lake and Galveston Bay, southeast of Houston, and they donated it to Rice with the understanding that it was to be used for the space center. The university was close to Ellington and right on Clear Lake, where a barge dock could be built to move massive rockets to the space center for testing.

Once the decision was made to place the center in Houston, the move went quickly. By November 1, 1961, NASA already had space in Houston. The management of Gulfgate Shopping Center (at the intersection of Interstate 45 and Interstate 610) donated three thousand square feet of floor space at the mall. The advance party from Langley was primarily concerned with finding temporary facilities to house the Manned Spaceflight Center. The Clear Lake property was a cattle pasture. The buildings closest to it were the Outpost, a ramshackle icehouse at the intersection of two country roads, and the abandoned West Mansion. Until the permanent NASA campus by Clear Lake was completed, facilities needed to be found in Southeast Houston or Pasadena. Some space could be found at Ellington, but it was an air force base with its own priorities and missions. Since NASA was a civilian agency, an Ellington headquarters was unsatisfactory.

The Farnsworth & Chambers Building off Wayside Drive in Southeast Houston was available. It was built in 1956–57 to serve as the headquarters of Farnsworth & Chambers, a construction company. When it built, the Farnsworth & Chambers Building was six miles from Houston's central business district in a bucolic suburban setting. Richard Farnsworth and Dunbar Chambers wanted to make a statement with their new headquarters, so they hired MacKie and Kamrath, a Houston-based architectural firm known for their Frank Lloyd Wright–inspired modernist designs. The architects delivered a one-story design that was covered in concrete and pale green Arizona quartzite. The building was flat-roofed and featured deep canopies and a large portico at the main entrance. It was striking, but Farnsworth & Chambers occupied it only briefly. A few months after the building was finished, Dunbar Chambers was killed in a hunting accident, and without him, the company faltered and slid into collapse. In 1961, the building was sold to Oscar Lee Gragg, an independent Texas oilman. Gragg, in turn, leased the building to NASA to serve as its headquarters. The Manned Spaceflight Center had a new home.

The MSC's public information office moved to the Farnsworth & Chambers Building in December 1961. The January 24, 1962 issue of *Space News Roundup*, the biweekly newsletter of the Manned Spacecraft

When NASA's move to Houston was announced, the site for what became the Manned Spacecraft Center was a cow pasture and was formerly a part of the West Ranch. This meant that NASA needed temporary quarters until construction finished. *Courtesy of the National Aerospace and Space Administration (NASA).*

Center, featured a full-page photo spread of activities in the building. The Houston site director, Martin Byrnes, was pictured working at his desk in his Farnsworth & Chambers Building office. Another photograph captured Robert Gilruth, the director of the Manned Spacecraft Center, hosting a delegation of visiting congressional representatives in the building's executive conference room.

Meanwhile, the MSC's move to Houston accelerated like a rocket leaving the launch pad. It started out slow, with just eleven employees moving to Houston in the first week of November 1961. By the end of January 1962, the MSC had over 200 employees in Houston. By April 1962, Houston's population of MSC employees reached 400, and in July, it reached 1,700. Among those moving to Houston that month was Robert Gilruth, who transferred from an office in Langley to a new one in the Farnsworth & Chambers Building. The MSC had so completely taken over Houston that

Space News Roundup moved to Houston in April, publishing its first Houston-bylined issue on April 18, 1962. The Farnsworth & Chambers Building was a great deal smaller than the multistory goliath that was built at the permanent site, but it was big enough for the MSC at its startup. It served as the MSC's temporary headquarters building for two years and four months.

Besides providing office space for Center Director Gilruth and his staff, the building briefly served as the astronaut office, which housed NASA's astronaut corps. At the time, there were only seven astronauts, the Mercury 7: Carpenter, Cooper, Glenn, Grissom, Schirra, Shepard and Slayton. Big decisions were made in that building. The orbital Mercury flights were managed out of the Farnsworth & Chambers Building. The decisions on who made the cut for the second class of astronauts—called the Next Nine—were made there. A high-tech communications room was installed there that contained everything that a 1963 version of a PowerPoint ranger could desire, including special audio and video links that allowed messages from the president to be broadcast and for MSC management to watch launches from Cape Canaveral. A lot of ordinary things happened there, too. What became the Johnson Space Center (JSC) Federal Credit was organized and housed there until March 1964. The building was also the site of blood drives, classes and organization meetings.

However, the Farnsworth & Chamber Building's glory days were fleeting. Its doom was sealed on December 3, 1962, when the contract for the construction of the first round of buildings at the Clear Lake site was signed. Among those covered by the contract was Building 2, a multistory building intended as the new project management building. (Building 1 was the Auditorium.) The contract was signed at a ceremony at the Farnsworth & Chambers Building. Ground was broken for Building 2 in early 1963. By July, the construction was going well; nine of the building's eleven stories had been framed. The building was complete by January 1964, and MSC's personnel began moving into it in February 1964. The first contingent to leave the Farnsworth & Chambers Building moved into Building 2 on March 4. This group included the Center Medical Operations, Credit Union, and Program Analysis and Resources Management Division. On March 6, they were joined by the director and his staff and the entirety of MSC's headquarters.

By March 11, the move was complete, and the Farnsworth & Chambers Building was empty. By June, all of MSC's personnel had moved onto the Clear Lake campus. It continued to maintain its offices and facilities at Ellington, but NASA terminated its leases on civilian buildings. Over

One of the first buildings built at NASA's Houston campus was the Project Management Building. This picture shows the building under construction, after framing was completed. This building replaced the Farnsworth & Chambers Building as the Manned Spacecraft Center's headquarters by March 1964. *Courtesy of the National Aerospace and Space Administration (NASA).*

the next twelve years, the Farnsworth & Chambers Building slipped into obscurity. Meanwhile, the Project Management Building had just started to experience its glory days. The Manned Spacecraft Center was run out of that building during the Gemini and Apollo projects, and it remains the JSC's headquarters today. It was still Building 2 when Armstrong spoke from the moon's surface, but the Project Management Building eventually swapped numbers with the Auditorium, becoming NASA Building 1. The Auditorium became Building 2, and for several years, JSC's Visitor's Center. (According to old JSC employees, the renumbering was done because an early space center director wanted his office in Building 1.)

In 1976, the Houston Parks and Recreation Department needed a new headquarters, so Gragg sold the Farnsworth & Chambers Building to the City of Houston. The following year, Gragg donated the surrounding acreage to the city for use as a park. The park was named Gragg Park, and

The Farnsworth & Chambers Building was purchased by the Houston Parks and Wildlife Department and was renamed the Gragg Building after Oscar Lee Gragg, who owned the building when NASA rented it. Today, it is the headquarters for Houston Parks and Wildlife. *Photograph by author.*

the Farnsworth & Chambers Building was renamed the Gragg Building. It served as the headquarters for Houston Parks and Recreation until 2008. By then, the building had become grungy. It had also been built in an era when carcinogenic building materials were the norm; it was too hazardous for occupation and required environmental remediation. Houston Parks and Recreation moved out while the building went through a fourteen-month reconstruction. The interior was gutted, and the building was rebuilt to LEED Gold standards. It was more of a rehabilitation than a restoration.

The building was reoccupied by the Houston Parks and Recreation Department in 2011. Its NASA heritage was acknowledged by the rebuild, and it was listed as a City of Houston Protected Landmark, a Recorded Texas Historic Landmark and has a Texas Historical Commission marker at the site. But its importance remains a far cry from what it was during the days when it was the home of the astronauts and rocket scientists of NASA who worked on Project Mercury.

11.

THE LOST ASTROWORLD

When former Harris County judge and Houston mayor Roy Mark Hofheinz ramrodded construction of the Astrodome, he called it the eighth Wonder of the World. In 1965, when the Astrodome opened, it was the first domed sports stadium to ever be built. The Astrodome was only a part of his larger vision, which he called the Astrodomain. In addition to the stadium, Hofheinz planned to build a massive shopping mall under a Buckminster Fuller enclosed dome, a hotel complex with hotels for every budget (from luxury five-star hotels to bargain motels) and a massive amusement park. However, Hofheinz's grand plan was never fully realized. The shopping center was never built. The hotel complex became known as Astro Village, and it had four lodgings when it was completed: a Holiday Inn, a Sheraton, a Howard Johnson's Motor Lodge and Restaurant and the AstroWorld Hotel, which contained the most expensive suite in the world in the 1960s.

AstroWorld, the amusement park, was also completed, and for nearly fifty years, it was one of Houston's most recognizable landmarks. AstroWorld was opened three years after the Astrodome, and in many ways, it was the crown jewel of Hofheinz's Astrodomain. The park filled fifty-seven acres of a 116-acre that site Hofheinz had purchased right across the Interstate 610 Loop from AstroWorld. It was opened on June 1, 1968, and was all things 1960s. It was named AstroWorld to celebrate Houston's new space industry, as the Manned Space Center—today's Johnson Space Center—had just been opened a few years earlier.

The park was built around an international theme, with sections of the park devoted to geographic themes. There was Americana Square that had a Norman Rockwell–like portrayal of life in the United States. The Alpine Valley section of the park had a Swiss theme and featured one of the park's signature rides: the Astroway, a skyway ride imported from Switzerland. The park's European Village featured a French taxi. The Plaza de Fiesta was a nod toward Central and South America and included a jungle ride. Oriental Corner took visitors to the then-exotic Far East. And AstroWorld's Western Junction transported folks to the nineteenth-century American West. Visitors could reach Western Junction by taking the 610 Limited, a steam locomotive that pulled historic cars from the 1870s. The concept may sound cheesy today, but back in the 1960s—before jumbo jets made international travel accessible to the average person—AstroWorld gave Houstonians the opportunity to experience different cultures and maybe get a little geographic education while they were being entertained.

In addition to the train and sky ride, AstroWorld's original collection of rides included a massive carousel, the Alpine Sleigh Ride, a double Ferris wheel, a scrambler, a spider ride, a sports car ride and bumper boats. The Alpine Sleigh Ride was a roller coaster that took passengers past fake glaciers and waterfalls. In keeping with the space theme, the double Ferris wheel was called the AstroWheel, and the scrambler was called the

This image shows AstroWorld as it appeared in the 1970s. Its dominant "world village" theme can be seen, expressed most obviously by the globe sculpture, in the park's central plaza. *Photograph by John H. Smith.*

A glipse of AstroWorld in 1977. With over fifty rides, visitors could fill most of a day if they rode each one. *Photograph by John H. Smith.*

Orbiter. The park also had a ride called the AstroNeedle; it was a tower with a double-deck gyro platform that traveled up a tall pole and rotated twice before reaching the top.

The most remarkable part of the park was its construction and the features that were built into it. Before construction started, the site was a swamp. Over 600,000 cubic yards of dirt were trucked in to fill the swamp, elevate the park and improve the land's drainage. Over ten thousand trees were planted for landscaping at the site, along with flower beds and decorative foliage. A pedestrian bridge was built over Interstate 610 to link AstroWorld with the Astrodome so that overflow parking for one facility could be handled by the parking lot of the other. An elevated monorail system was conceptualized as a way to link AstroWorld with the rest of the Astrodomain, but it was never constructed.

Hofheinz wanted to find some way to convince crowds to visit AstroWorld and wander around outside during the summer in Houston. It gets plenty hot in Houston during the summer, especially when the high heat is combined with high humidity. In some cities, you can fry an egg on the pavement in the summertime, but if you crack an egg on the pavement in Houston on a hot summer's day, it will most likely fry. Hofheinz's solution to this was outdoor air conditioning. Miles of pipes were placed under the park to carry chilled water to picnic areas, queue areas, open-air restaurants and shops and other large, open spaces. While the system was not perfect, it worked surprisingly well.

Hofheinz invested $25 million into building the amusement park of his dreams. He projected that the park would have an annual attendance of 1.6 million visitors once things got rolling. AstroWorld proved to be popular but not as popular as Hofheinz had planned. On opening weekend, 50,000 visitors came through the gate. Admission was $4.50 for adults, $3.50 for children and $0.50 for parking, so a father, mother and three children could attend the park for just $20.00. Tickets admitted visitors to every ride in the park, and with over fifty rides to choose from, they could spend an entire day there without taking the same ride twice. The park also hosted shows and concerts, so a family of five could get a day's worth of entertainment for less than a day's pay at the median family income for 1968. It was a good deal, and many took it in the late 1960s and 1970s. Hofheinz had achieved one goal: he had created a family-friendly attraction in Houston.

AstroWorld continued to grow over the next few years. Two rides, including a log-flume ride, were added to Oriental Corner in 1969. In 1970, an eighth area called Fun Island was opened with two additional attractions. A ninth area was added in 1972, which was called Country Fair. Where Fun Island had been added to a lagoon between two existing areas, Country Fair actually expanded the park from its original fifty-seven acres to seventy-five acres.

Roy Hofheinz suffered a stroke in 1970, which left him confined to a wheelchair. While AstroWorld did well in the early 1970s, Hofheinz's investment in the Astrodomain did not do as well. The inflation rate was soaring during the 1970s, and Hofheinz had borrowed heavily to develop Astrodomain. By 1975, the project was $38 million in debt, which cost Hofheinz his control over the investment; two creditors took over the business in 1975. In the same year, the Hofheinz family leased AstroWorld to the Six Flags Corporation. The lease included an option to buy the park, so Six Flags purchased AstroWorld in 1976, making it the first existing park to be purchased by the chain. Six Flags had opened its first park, Six Flags Over Texas, in Arlington in 1961. By 1975, Six Flags had built two other amusement parks: Six Flags Over Georgia in Atlanta and Six Flags Over Mid-America in St. Louis, Missouri.

Over the next ten years, the change in ownership benefited AstroWorld. In 1975, a Coney Island–style wooden roller coaster was added to the park. Before construction on the roller coaster was started, management considered buying Coney Island's Cyclone and moving it to Texas, but they opted to build a bigger, faster and taller copy of the ride instead. The park was in Texas, and *everything* has to be bigger in Texas. The resulting ride was called the Texas Cyclone. It was a landmark that was visible from Interstate 610, and for a time, it was rated as the nation's number one wooden roller coaster. Greezed Lightning, a metal roller coaster with an eighty-foot-tall loop, was added in 1978. The ride would go from a dead stop to a speed of sixty miles per hour in just four seconds.

A number of other rides were also added to the park in the early 1908s, including Thunder River, XLR-8 (a suspended roller coaster), the Skyscreamer (a free-fall ride that was added in 1982) and Water World (a fifteen-acre water park that was added in 1983). An outdoor stage facility, the Southern Star Amphitheater, was added to the park in 1985. In 1986, a ride called Looping Starship was also added to the park. Initially, the ride was called Challenger as an homage to NASA's Space Shuttle program. But after the Space Shuttle *Challenger*—the ride's namesake—was destroyed shortly after launch on January 28, 1986, AstroWorld's management quietly renamed the ride. AstroWorld's growth continued into the 1990s. The first stand-up roller coaster in Texas, a Batman-themed ride called Batman: The Escape, was added in the 1990s. This decade also saw the addition of an indoor roller-coaster, a pipeline shuttle coaster and a looping roller coaster called the Texas Tornado.

The Texas Cyclone roller coaster was clearly visible from Loop I-610 as you drove past the park. This wooden roller coaster was considered the United States' number one wooden roller coaster for several years after it was built. *Photograph by John H. Smith.*

Two generations of Houston children came to AstroWorld. When the baby boomers of the 1960s grew up, they brought their children to AstroWorld in the 1980s and 1990s. For many teenaged Houstonians, getting a driver's license and a season pass to AstroWorld was a rite of passage. But that all came to a sudden end in 2005, when Six Flags announced that it would be shutting down AstroWorld at the end of the 2005 season. It was AstroWorld's thirty-seventh—and last—season. October 30 was AstroWorld's traditional annual closing date. The only difference between October 30, 2005, and the previous thirty-six closing dates was that the park was shut down for good that time. Over the winter, the park was dismantled; the Texas Cyclone was demolished (with the exception of one section that was preserved for a future museum exhibit), rides—including Greezed Lightning and the Texas Tornado—were relocated and the cars from several rides were either sent to other Six Flags parks or sold to other corporations.

Many Houstonians were left with questions about what happened to the park. Many AstroWorld fans theorize about conspiracies that may have existed to close the park. But there was no grand plan. Rather, several factors converged to doom AstroWorld. The park's first problem was that there were simply fewer children to go to AstroWorld at the start of the new millennium. The average family in 1968 consisted of 3.6 people; it was normal for young married couples to have two or three children. Even families with four to six children were not unusual. By 1995, the average household had shrunk to just 3.2 people. By 2005, when AstroWorld closed, it had dropped even lower to 3.1. Families with one or two children had become the norm, and single-parent families had also become common. Families with children also had less disposable income, and fewer teens were buying season passes.

Another problem for the park was that the tastes in Houston had also changed. AstroWorld's world village theme was cutting edge in 1968, but by 2000, it started to feel outdated. Cheap airfares meant Houstonians did not have to go to AstroWorld to experience Europe, Asia or South America; they could just buy economy tickets and fly to those places. AstroWorld compensated by replacing exotic locales with superhero themes and Fright Nights, but they were limited by the park's original plans. While space exploration was the cool thing in 1968, by 2000, it was old hat. Video games had also made amusement park rides seem dull to the Millennials who were growing up in the late 1990s and first years of the twenty-first century. Amusement park customers tended to be older twenty-somethings rather than teens or children and their

Today, the site of AstroWorld is an empty field. The walkway over I-610 still exists, but the parking lot is overgrown with weeds. *Photograph by Marianne Avioliotis.*

parents. Kemah's Boardwalk, which opened in 1998, was catered more to their tastes. The rides there were not as extreme as AstroWorld's, but you could get drinks and meals that were a cut above what was available at AstroWorld.

Houston's sports teams also stopped using the Astrodome in 1999. The Houston Oilers football franchise moved to Tennessee in 1996, and the Houston Astros baseball team abandoned the Astrodome for Minute Maid Park in 1999. When the Houston Texans football team started playing in 2002, they passed over the Astrodome for NRG Stadium. The loss of major-league teams playing at the Astrodome deprived AstroWorld of its extra parking revenues.

The land on which AstroWorld was located had also soared in value in the early twenty-first century. In 1968, the land was a greenfield development located on the edge of town. By 2005, the park was in the center of Houston's South Side, and some estimates valued its land at $150 million. Six Flags parent company was looking to reduce debt. AstroWorld had a large payroll (approximately 1,200 employees, including seasonal help) and shrinking revenue, and it was seemingly worth a fortune if the land was sold. Closing it seemed smart. By 2006, a bare open field had replaced AstroWorld, and the land was sold for $77 million—just half of the expected value. The park was gone and there was no reviving it. While several development projects for the land have been floated since 2005, AstroWorld remains an empty field. Today's teens, who are becoming old enough to get their first driver's licenses, have always remembered the location as an empty field.

12.

LIGHTER THAN AIR

Few corporate symbols are as recognizable as the Goodyear Blimp. Since 1925, when Goodyear launched *Pilgrim*, its first advertising blimp, these aerial billboards have sold Goodyear tires.

A blimp is an adman's ultimate fantasy. With the exception of advertising agencies and their clients, few people love billboards. Yes, they are effective—otherwise, businesses would not pay to advertise on them—but most people consider billboards to be eyesores and want them gone—but this is not the case when the billboard is a blimp. People do not think of blimps as eyesores, even when they serve as floating billboards. Blimps are cool. Any lighter-than-air craft is cool. Maybe people are attracted to the spectacle of something so large defying gravity. Or maybe they are attracted by a return to childhood memories of playing with helium-filled balloons. For whatever reason, people flock outdoors to watch blimps when they are in the neighborhood. Not only do neighborhoods welcome blimps but some even fight over the opportunity to have a blimp visit them.

Recently, some marketing departments have tried to capture the same attraction with hot air balloons; at least one real estate franchise uses a hot-air balloon as its trademark. Houston also hosted the Ballunar Liftoff Festival, an event that was once held annually to celebrate the anniversary of the first lunar landing. But balloons are hostage to the wind; you cannot get them to go where you want them to go. A blimp is self-propelled and can hover at will. Blimps can even serve as a platform for photography—for football games or auto racing. At these events, advertisers know that there are between 50,000 and 150,000 people present to look at their floating billboard, which is not bad. While blimps are effective, they are not a cheap form of advertising. Blimps need an airbase to operate out of, a hangar to be stored in and a shop and fuel for their engines. Standard airports can be used to store blimps, but blimps and aircraft do not play well together. Blimps take a more leisurely approach to air travel than even a light airplane, much less a passenger jet.

Goodyear is not the only corporation to advertise with blimps. Fujifilm had one back in the day, when most cameras still used film. MetLife and DirecTV also have advertising blimps. With the inclusion of the Goodyear stable, there are about a dozen active advertising blimps worldwide. Yet, Goodyear is the corporation best known for its blimps. The company not only uses blimps, but it is also a major manufacturer of them. Goodyear also has its own set of blimp bases that its airships operate from. Once, there was one near Houston in Spring, Texas.

In 1959, Goodyear developed a new blimp design: the GZ-19 (GZ stood for Goodyear-Zeppelin—their original partner in lighter-than-air construction). The blimp had a 132,000-cubic-foot envelope that was filled with helium gas—about 50 percent larger than the earlier Goodyear Blimps. The first GZ-19 was named *Mayflower* after an America's Cup racing yacht. It was the first blimp to have what Goodyear called its "Skytacular" sign, a four-color running night sign. The sign was so successful that Goodyear expanded the concept. In 1969, Goodyear built two blimps with a new, larger GZ-20 design. These blimps had a 202,700-cubic-foot envelope and more powerful engines. These new blimps were able to carry a bigger and better version of the "Skytacular," which Goodyear dubbed the "Super-Skytacular." The two GZ-20 blimps were named *America* and *Columbia*.

To take advantage of the Sunbelt's growth , Goodyear put a blimp base near Houston. The company chose a spot next to Interstate 45 in Spring, Texas. Why Spring? Well, the City of Houston and the Federal Aviation Administration had something to do with that. Goodyear first proposed the placement of a blimp base in Houston in 1968. The FAA was concerned about mixing blimp traffic with jet traffic. At that time, the major airport for Houston was William P. Hobby Airport (a name that was one year old in 1967) in Southeast Houston. The city was also home to Ellington, south and east of Hobby, but that was an air force base that would not be opened to commercial traffic for another fifteen years. The city was also still building Houston Intercontinental Airport (today, it is called George W. Bush Intercontinental) on Houston's far North Side. At the time, Houston

Between 1969 and 1992, Goodyear maintained a blimp base north of Houston, near Spring, Texas. In this image, the ground crew, which included summer workers from Spring High School, are helping to capture and maneuver one of the Goodyear Blimps during ground operations. *Photograph by Marianne Dyson.*

Intercontinental was being built to replace Hobby and was scheduled to open in 1969. The FAA wanted to keep Goodyear's blimp operations well away from all of these fields, as the conditions around them could have been hazardous for all aircraft. The City of Houston also objected; they did not want to mix jets and blimps at their airports. The air force certainly did not want blimps operating from Ellington Air Force Base, which was then home to a squadron of supersonic fighter jets. The agency told Goodyear to try either Houston's West or East Side.

Goodyear balked at both suggestions. Houston's East Side was home to the petrochemical industry, which was clustered around the Houston Ship Channel. At that time, air quality laws were a lot looser than today, and the

Some lucky souls got to ride the Goodyear Blimps during their stays in Houston. These passengers included politicians, news media representatives, special guests and (as in the case with this pair) relatives of Goodyear employees. *Photograph by Marianne Dyson.*

air there had a distinctive aroma. The locals claimed it "smelled like money." Goodyear officials were concerned that a concentrated exposure to the smell would harm the blimps' large rubberized envelopes. Goodyear officials were also uninterested in Galveston County or Brazoria County, because of their proximity to the Gulf of Mexico; they were worried about potential hurricane damage. There had been a U.S. Navy blimp base near Hitchcock, Texas, which is near the Gulf Coast, but there had been a war on when it was built. U-boats were a larger concern for them than hurricanes. So, Goodyear held out for a location north of Houston, and after negotiations, the FAA and Goodyear agreed to a location in Spring. The location was to the north and west of Intercontinental's runways, and it was off the flight path of aircraft that were taking off from or landing on runways 8/26 or 15/33. Goodyear agreed to keep the blimps away from Intercontinental's pattern, so Houston removed its objections and the FAA granted approval.

When the site was chosen, the area was rural. Technically, it was a private airfield with a 1,700-foot-long unpaved runway. If the engine was cut out of a Cessna, its pilot may have been able to land there. A Piper Cub may have possibly taken off from the runway, but it was not intended for straight-winged aircraft—it was designed for blimps. The airfield had two mooring towers for blimps in its center, and it had a massive hangar in its northwest corner that always caught the attentions of visitors. A GZ-20 is nearly 200 feet long and 60 feet tall; to contain one, one would need a building that stands seven stories high and is nearly the length of a football field. Additionally, the hangar had to be capable of withstanding hurricane-force winds, so the girders that comprised the framework, as well as the hangar door, exuded the stability of a battleship.

The blimp base opened in 1969, when Goodyear sent its brand-new blimp, *America*, to Houston. The *America* came complete with its own ghost story. Before 1982, when the blimp was refurbished, it used the gondola from the "Ghost Blimp," a World War II blimp that returned from an antisubmarine patrol without its crew. For the next twenty-five years, both *America* and the base were Houston landmarks. Locals often saw *America* cruising over parts of Houston while it was either traveling to a destination, participating in a Houston event or being used by its pilots for practice. The blimp base itself was easily noticeable from the highway. When driving down Interstate 45 from areas in the north—Dallas and Huntsville—the sight of the hangar would announce to drivers that they were nearing Houston. The base was also something for drivers to watch for as they took Interstate 45 to the lakes north of Houston or to (while it was briefly open) Hanna-Barbara Land—the northern suburbs' answer to AstroWorld. When the blimps were flying, cars would park on the interstate's service drives to watch them. Since the base was across the interstate from Spring High School, it also provided after-school and summer employment for an entire generation of students. The blimps flying in and out of the base also gave daydreaming students something to watch as they sat at their desks, bored with class.

Over the next twenty-five years, many Houstonians and Texans caught rides on *America* and *Columbia*, the two blimps Goodyear operated out of their Houston blimp base. The blimps were not commercial vehicles, so their passengers generally fell into one of three categories: politicians, media

Technically, the Goodyear Blimp Base was a private airfield; although, it is shown on this 1980s U.S. Geological Survey sectional map as a "Landing Field (blimp)." It can be seen at the top of the map, to the left of the red line marking Interstate 45. The blimp base's hangars and landing pads are marked. *Author's collection.*

figures and Goodyear employees and their families. If a local political figure expressed interest in taking a ride, Goodyear was glad to accommodate them under the guise of community relations in order to educate local lawmakers about the value of blimps. Similarly, giving a newshawk a ride aboard one of the blimps provided Goodyear with great publicity; their rides were almost always followed by enthusiastic articles about the blimp. Many famous Houston media figures took the opportunity to take a ride, as it was a fun story to research, print and broadcast.

As with any type of aircraft, training and practice flights were required to keep the crews' flight certifications current. This meant that there were a lot of noncommercial flights of the blimps that Goodyear employees—and their relatives—could occasionally catch rides on. The blimps were flying anyway, and it was good for company morale. Back then, anyone with the money for a trip on the Concorde could fly on a supersonic jet but riding on a blimp gave a person bragging rights.

But alas, all good things must come to an end. Houston's relentless march north along the Interstate 45 and US-59 corridors encroached on the blimp base by the late 1980s. By 1991, there were strip shopping centers across the street from the base to the north and west. And property values along the interstate were soaring higher than a blimp's ceiling. Feeling crowded, Goodyear closed the base in 1992. This was a cost-cutting move for Goodyear as well. The blimps of the 1990s were much more capable than the blimps of the 1960s; they could travel farther and faster. Fewer blimp bases were needed, and the land value of the Spring base had soared. Goodyear not only cut overhead by eliminating its Texas base—it actually made a tidy profit off the land. After the Texas base was closed, *America* was relocated to Wingfoot Lake Airship Base outside of Akron, Ohio. The blimp was decommissioned and replaced a few years later.

The quadrilateral of roads marking the boundaries of the blimp base now contain a shopping center. Today, a hardware store occupies the space that was once taken by the blimp hangar. This image shows the concrete floor of the former hangar. *Photograph by John Lardas.*

The base stood empty for a while, but shortly after closing its airship operations in Houston, Goodyear rented the hangar to the rock band Genesis. The band used the hangar as a practice venue during their 1992 North America tour; after all, it was almost as big as a small stadium. Eventually, Goodyear dismantled the hangar at the Spring base in 1994. For a while, the girders could be seen from the interstate, like the ribcage of an extinct dinosaur, but they, too, eventually came down. The hangar was relocated to San Diego, although it also no longer appears to be used. Goodyear's remaining active blimp bases are located in Wingfoot Lake, Ohio; Carson, California and Pompano Beach, Florida. Today, no trace remains of the Goodyear Blimp Base in Spring, Texas; the site is now occupied by a Lowe's and a Home Depot.

13.

MIDNIGHT FOR AN
URBAN COWBOY

Despite the intellectual veneer of Houston's space, medical and high-tech industries, Houston has always been a blue-collar town. Houston's shipping, chemical and petroleum industries produce a spate of jobs for those who are willing to work hard with their hands. They are not office jobs; they involve physical labor, and often, a degree of danger. They can be dull, but more often, they require brains and attention to detail along with hard work, even if they do not require a four-year degree. These jobs pay well, too. When billion-dollar capital investments are involved, bosses are unlikely to stint pay in order to get reliable workers. An automated petrochemical plant employs hundreds of workers, if not tens of thousands of workers. In the long run, plant managers find it is cheaper to pay to get the best. For these reasons, in the 1960s, there was no city that was more blue-collar than Houston—except for maybe Detroit. A lot of the workers in these industries were originally from the Texas countryside and grew up on farms. They were no strangers to hard work, and the plants, factories and oil rigs around Houston paid them a lot better than farming would.

When Houston's blue-collar workers were off the clock, they liked to blow off steam. Many of them would stop off at an icehouse on the way home for a cold beer, and they often went with their coworkers. An icehouse was not a place that manufactured ice; rather, it was an open-air store that sold beer chilled with ice. Icehouses did start out just selling ice, but they also started selling groceries and beer as the twentieth century progressed. After a while, no one needed to buy ice anymore, and icehouse owners noticed that

Houston's 1970s and 1980s honky-tonk scene was an outgrowth of its petrochemical industry. The blue-collar workers employed at the plants worked hard during the week and wanted to play hard during the evenings and on the weekends. *Courtesy of the Library of Congress.*

their hottest-selling product was their cold, ice-chilled beer. Smart icehouse owners set up picnic tables under awnings outside of their buildings, cut out the groceries (except for munchies and burgers to go with the beer) and served as neighborhood social clubs for hourly workers.

Other blue-collar Houstonians would head for a honky-tonk to get some music and dancing with their beer. A honky-tonk was not just a bar that sold beer; it also featured live music. Honky-tonk music was county music; it was a loud, two-beat sound that was easy to dance to. Piano, steel guitar, fiddle, bass and nasal vocals were often featured, and rhythm trumped melody and harmony. The words to songs had to be understandable, and their themes often centered on drinking, love (generally love gone bad) and women (including hookers), as well as the classic standbys like dogs, trains, Mama, the farm, riding, pickup trucks and the other accompaniments of country life. When Friday came, Houston's blue-collar crowd cut loose for the weekend. They worked hard and played hard, and the weekend was the time for play in this uniquely Texas culture.

The icehouse and honky-tonk scene emerged after World War II, and just continued to grow over the next thirty years. Honky-tonks were scattered all over Houston, wherever there were working-class neighborhoods. The greatest concentration of honky-tonks could be found in the eastern and southeastern reaches of the greater Houston metropolitan area in towns like Galena Park, Deer Park, La Porte and Pasadena. These towns were where the chemical plants and refineries were clustered and were where many of the workers at those plants lived. The largest, and ultimately most famous, of these honky-tonks was Gilley's in Pasadena, Texas, which was opened in 1970.

Sherwood Cryer was an East Texas boy who served in the army air force during and immediately after World War II. He moved to Pasadena to work for Shell Oil after the war ended. Bored with life as a welder, Cryer began running nightclubs, convenience stores and a vending machine service. In the 1960s, Cryer owned a club in Pasadena called Shelley's, but had closed it down. During the 1950s and 1960s, it seemed like half of Louisiana was moving to Houston for work at the petrochemical plants, and the other half followed them to provide entertainment. In 1970, Mickey Gilley was a relatively recent arrival in the Houston area. He was from Louisiana, so music was in his blood. His cousins included Louisiana country singer Jerry Lee Lewis and Louisiana evangelist Jimmy Swaggart.

By the late 1960s, Gilley was performing in the Houston nightclub scene when Cryer saw him and liked his performance. Cryer decided to reopen Shelley's, using Gilley as its headline act and public face, and he pitched the

While Gilley's claimed the title of the world's largest and best honky-tonk in the 1970s, when the new decade started, it found itself surpassed by Fort Worth, Texas's Billy-Bob's. *Courtesy of the Library of Congress.*

idea of a partnership to the young singer. Although Mickey wanted to name the nightclub Den of Sin, Cryer had already decided to call the club Gilley's after its namesake owner. The club's building was huge; it had probably been built as an industrial warehouse and seemed large enough to serve as a B-52 hangar. The parking lot was unpaved, and the floor was bare concrete, except for the dance area, which was covered with parquet wood. The building had a basic drop-down ceiling made of acoustic tiles. Some of the tiles were water-stained from water dripping through the leaky metal roof, and others were simply missing. Through the gaps, you could see the building's wiring. Getting to the restrooms involved a long hike, unless you were already at the back of the building. The building's furnishings were basic, and its counters were often made up from stacked beer cartons. The place had a huge stage for the live bands that performed there, along with showers for truckers and sections for those looking for entertainment other than dancing.

These additional sections included a pool hall filled with billiard tables, a shooting gallery and an arcade area filled with pinball machines, punching-bag machines and a mechanical bull. The bull became an icon in the 1980s, but in the 1970s, it was just another way for blue-collar Houstonians to let off steam. The bull simulated a rodeo ride, with the risk of getting tossed—but without the risk of getting trampled. Originally, it was surrounded by dirty white mattresses to cushion those pitched off the ride. There are rumors that those mattresses came from a Mexican brothel just across the border. The cost of shipping even free mattresses from the Texas border made that idea ridiculous; it is more likely that they were discarded from a low-rent, Houston-area motel. However, the Mexican brothel rumor sounded better to the type of kickers that came to Gilley's.

Gilley's music at this time was pure 1970s country. Everyone who was anyone in country music at the time played a gig at Gilley's. Featured acts included Charlie Daniels, Loretta Lynn, Ernest Tubb, Emmylou Harris,, Roseanne Cash and many more. Mickey Gilley was also racking up a string of number one country hits, including "Room Full of Roses," "Chains of Love," "Honky Tonk Memories," "She's Pulling Me Back Again" and "Here Comes the Hurt Again." In 1977, a weekly radio show was started called *Live From Gilley's*. It would eventually be carried by five hundred radio stations, including Armed Forces Radio.

Gilley's was open seven days a week, from 10:00 am to 2:00 am., and its motto was "We Doze, but We Never Close." If you did not have anywhere to go on Thanksgiving, you could go to Gilley's. At Gilley's,

After Gilley's defaulted on its property taxes, the land was seized by the Pasadena Independent School District. The school district built Marshall Kendrick Middle School on the site and placed the school building in the rodeo arena area. *Photograph by author.*

patrons could get cold beer, listen to hot country music, shoot some pool, ride the bull, dance the two-step with a honky-tonk angel (who always got better looking at closing time) and get into a fistfight or two if they really wanted to let off steam. Gilley's fit the needs of enough folks during the 1970s to be filled every weeknight and overflowing on weekends. The *Guinness Book of World Records* recognized Gilley's as "the world's largest nightclub." Then, the serpent entered this honky-tonk paradise and Gilley's got discovered.

Texas-born Aaron Latham was a journalist writing for East Coast magazines. In 1978, he wrote "The Ballad of the Urban Cowboy: America's Search for True Grit," an article about the Houston nightclub scene in general—and Gilley's in particular—for the September 12 issue of *Esquire*. The article attracted the interest of Hollywood, just as Sherwood Cryer had hoped when he sold Latham on writing the article. Latham sold a script to Hollywood based on the article, and it became the basis for the movie *Urban Cowboy*, which was released in 1980 and stars John Travolta and Debra

Winger. Travolta played Bud, a petroleum plant worker, and Winger played a cowgirl named Sissy.

The movie depicts a boy-meets-girl love story and uses Gilley's as the background for most of its action. Much of the movie was filmed in Houston and Pasadena, and some of Gilley's regulars even appeared in the movie as extras or named cast members. The movie became a monster hit. Travolta was at the top of his career coming off *Saturday Night Fever* and *Grease*, but by 1980, disco had grown stale. The American public was seeking a new sound, and thanks to *Urban Cowboy*, honky-tonk country became that new sound. Soon, everyone was wearing cowboy boots, jeans and snap-button shirts, sucking down long-neck beers and dancing to the "Cotton-Eyed Joe," just like Bud and Sissy. These original markers of blue-collar plant workers were adopted by bicoastal stockbrokers and lawyers; "country" became a national craze and one that would stick for nearly a decade, and honky-tonk bars, complete with bull-riding machines, popped up all over the United States.

Gilley's prospered. Just as everyone wanted to go to Rick's American Café in Casablanca in the 1940s, everyone wanted to go to Gilley's in the 1980s. The difference was that visitors could actually go to Gilley's. It soon became the most popular tourist spot in the Houston area—it was even more than the Johnson Space Center and AstroWorld. Because of this increase in business, Cryer and Gilley expanded the operation, adding souvenir shops and a rodeo arena that doubled as a motocross venue. Gilley's also went upscale, replacing the dirty mattresses with shiny red mats that were made from vinyl so they could be hosed off. The restrooms, however, were just as dirty, the parking lot remained dirt-covered and the ceiling tiles kept disappearing.

Gilley's lost its crown as the biggest nightclub in the nation in 1981, when Billy-Bob's opened in Fort Worth, Texas. The bar's regulars also started to disappear; the new crowd was too posh for the tastes of the blue-collar workers that packed the place prior to *Urban Cowboy*. Country music was transforming to fit the tastes of its larger, national audience, and it lost its twang and rough edges to a more popular sound. This style played well to a national audience but not to the regulars; they moved on to other places, where they could continue their rowdy ways without yielding to the upper-middle-class newcomers who were flocking to Gilley's.

Gilley's good times rolled through to the early 1980s. In 1984, it was named the best nightclub of the year by the Academy of Country Music before two disasters struck simultaneously: the 1980s oil bust and the passing of the country music craze. The new audience moved on to other sounds, and the old audience was simply struggling to keep their jobs. What disposable

Today, the only remaining part of Gilley's is the former recording studio. This abandoned concrete building is fenced off from the middle school. *Photograph by author.*

income they had was being spent at newer, cheaper places. Gilley's started on a downhill slide; it went slowly at first and then fell apart all at once. Cryer and Gilley began feuding over the upkeep and maintenance of the place. Mickey Gilley finally sued Cryer in 1988. Cryer lost the lawsuit and had to sign the club to over Gilley and pay him $17 million. Gilley ran the bar for another year until another legal action led to the club's demise in 1989. Then, in 1990, the club burned down; arson was suspected. The property, including the burned-out nightclub, rodeo arena and outbuildings, ultimately ended up in the hands of the Pasadena Independent School District in 1992. The property was prime acreage located on Spencer Highway, but PISD could not find a buyer. In 2005, the school district bulldozed everything and built a middle school on part of the property.

Gilley's had a second life but not in the Houston area. Throughout the 1990s, Mickey Gilley explored potential new locations for a Gilley's. In 2003, he opened Gilley's Dallas at 1135 South Lamar Street in Dallas. At 90,000 square feet, it is smaller than Billy-Bob's, but it has a mechanical bull, just like the original Gilley's.

14.

A REMARKABLE RANDALLS

Consider American supermarkets; they are ubiquitous, every neighborhood has one and there are often four or five of them within a few miles of anyone's home. Anyone can go to an American supermarket and get a marvelous assortment of food, including fresh vegetables, meat and dairy products, aisles of canned and dried goods and rows of frozen food. Most of them even have delis attached. Supermarkets even have more than food; they have aisles that contain cleaning supplies, hardware, paper products, basic auto supplies, and even clothes. No one in America thinks that this is in any way remarkable. Americans take it for granted that they can pop over to the supermarket and pick up everything they need for day-to-day living. That is, until a crisis, like a hurricane, earthquake or blizzard, comes through and deprives folks of their uninterrupted access to groceries. And it has been this way in the United States since the 1920s.

It was rarely that way in much of the world during the twentieth century. Frequently, only the elite had access to supermarkets, even in the industrial world. And these supermarkets rarely had the breadth of selection or even the quality of goods—especially with perishable meat, vegetables and dairy—that is available in modern American supermarkets. This rift between American supermarkets and the reality of the shopping experience in other nations set into motion actions that led to the collapse of one of the late twentieth century's two superpowers. An ordinary neighborhood supermarket in Houston, a Randalls at the corner of El Dorado and Highway 3 in Houston's Clear Lake area, was the starting point for a chain

Randalls was one of a number of grocery store chains that served the Houston area back in the 1980s. What made this Randalls special was Boris Yeltsin's unexpected visit in 1987. Before, it was an ordinary Texas grocery store. *Photograph by author.*

of events that culminated with a man standing on a tank in Moscow's Red Square and the disintegration of the Soviet Union.

In 1987, Boris Yeltsin was one of the rising stars of the Communist Party of the Soviet Union (CPSU). He had been appointed as the first secretary of the CPSU Moscow City Committee in 1985, effectively making him the "mayor" of Moscow. In the following two years, he made himself popular among Moscow's residents by touting himself as a populist political reformer and cracking down on corrupt politicians. In 1987, he resigned from the Politburo to protest the slow pace of Soviet reforms under Mikhail Gorbachev. It was an unprecedented move, as no one had ever *voluntarily* resigned from the Politburo before. It sealed his reputation as a reformer, even as it put his career into eclipse. Shortly after Gorbachev formed the Congress of People's Deputies and named it the Soviet Union's supreme legislative body in 1988, Yeltsin ran for office as the delegate to the Moscow district. In March 1989, he won the election and soon became the head of the pro-reform faction. It was during his time in that role that he made a visit to Houston as part of a bigger tour of the United States.

During his visit, Yeltsin toured Johnson Space Center. While Yeltsin was not a head of state, he was (at least in the eyes of the U.S. Department of State) another foreign politician, and an important one, since he was the head of a faction in the Soviet Congress of Deputies. As far as the United States government was concerned, Johnson Space Center, the headquarters for the United States' manned spaceflight program, was a must-see spot for any foreign visitor, especially one they wished to impress. On September 16, 1989, Yeltsin went on a VIP tour of Johnson Space Center. He got a tour of Mission Control in Building 30, but since he stopped by between Space Shuttle missions, he probably just saw an empty amphitheater of control consoles. Or, if he was really lucky, the flight control team may have been running a simulation as practice for the upcoming STS-34 mission that was scheduled to fly in October. (This mission would launch the *Galileo* satellite to Jupiter.) Regardless, it was probably not notably more impressive than the Soviet Union's manned mission flight control center in Moscow.

While he was there, Yeltsin also got to tour a mock-up of NASA's planned space station, which was then named *Freedom*. Development on the space station began in April 1984, but by 1989, the program was still in the design phase and the launch of the first element was scheduled for 1995. The hardware was only starting construction, and what Yeltsin saw was, essentially, a mock-up of the inhabited portions of the station and a model of the proposed design. The Soviet Union had been flying space stations since 1971, and at the time of Yeltsin's 1989 visit, the then-current Soviet space station, *Mir*, had been in orbit with a three-man crew for over three years. NASA's upcoming space station could not have impressed Yeltsin all that much. (*Freedom* was ultimately never built.)

Once his visit to Johnson Space Center was over, Yeltsin and his entourage boarded their limousines for a trip to Houston's Ellington Airfield, where Yeltsin took a flight to Miami, the next stop on his American tour. At that point, nothing he had seen provided any real indication of America's superiority. But as they were heading toward the Gulf Freeway on El Dorado Boulevard, Yeltsin spotted a Randalls supermarket at the corner of El Dorado and Highway 3. On an impulse, he ordered his driver to stop there. There was no apparent reason for Yeltsin to stop there; it was an ordinary American corner supermarket. Some unkind people claim that he saw a liquor store next to the Randalls and stopped to quench his thirst. But he went into the Randalls, not the liquor store next door. Perhaps he was bored; it is possible that he had been so unimpressed by his visit to NASA that he impulsively decided to confirm a dismal impression of America with an unscheduled stop at a random grocery store. Regardless, what happened next changed Yeltsin and, in turn, changed the world.

Yeltsin had been taken on a tour of NASA's Johnson Space Center as part of a delegation of Soviet dignitaries. Yeltsin left Johnson Space Center unimpressed with the United States' manned spaceflight capabilities in 1987. *Courtesy of the National Aerospace and Space Administration (NASA).*

The store was not what he expected. It was spotless and crowded with customers, but there were no long lines, even at checkout. Perhaps most surprising to Yeltsin was the self-service nature of the store. Customers did not ask for goods to be doled out by shopkeepers; they just picked what they needed from the shelves. The customers could even select what they wanted and were able to bypass the wilted vegetables and dented cans that might have been forced on them at a Soviet grocery. Even more amazing was the variety and quality of the goods that were available. There was not just one brand of cereal on the shelves, there were dozens. Even the shelves

Boris Yeltsin abandoned communism as a result of his experience at Randalls in 1987. This experience eventually led him to become the president of the independent Russian Federation. This photo shows him during his tenure as Russia's president in the 1990s. *Author's collection.*

with prosaic offerings of dried beans, rice and canned tomato sauce offered a choice of brands, sizes and styles. And everything in the store seemed new. What was even more remarkable to Yeltsin was the selection of fresh vegetables in the produce section, the wrapped and packaged meat in the meat department and the fresh fish that was available. Not only were the bins containing these goods completely filled, but the produce, meat, and fish in them were fresh as well. Then, there was the frozen goods section. Yeltsin was fascinated by the frozen pudding pops that were explosively popular with Americans in the 1980s.

Yeltsin spent twenty minutes at that Randalls, wandering the packed aisles, speaking to the shoppers and trying the cheese that was offered as a sample to customers. He asked the shoppers what they were buying, the cost of their groceries and whether they could get better bargains elsewhere. He marveled at the checkout counters and the polite and friendly staff. They were not just friendly to him; they were polite and friendly to all the other customers. He accepted a yellow rose that was offered to him by a customer who was trying to make him feel at home in Texas. Yeltsin even asked the store manager if there was specialized training to manage a store like this. When he left, the store gave him a small goodie bag to enjoy on his trip. After the visit, he told his entourage, "Even the Politburo doesn't have this choice. Not even Mr. Gorbachev."

This visit to Randalls was transformative. The image of row after row of the well-stocked aisles and their dozens of varieties amazed and depressed him. Yeltsin would later write in his autobiography:

When I saw those shelves crammed with hundreds, thousands of cans, cartons and goods of every possible sort, for the first time I felt quite frankly sick with despair for the Soviet people. That such a potentially super-rich country as ours has been brought to a state of such poverty! It is terrible to think of it.

He brooded about the visit on his flight to Miami; he sat motionless with his head in his hands. To him, the most shocking part of his visit was the realization that this was not a special store reserved for the elite at NASA. It was an ordinary corner supermarket that anyone could shop at. There were hundreds of these stores in Houston alone, and they were replicated in thousands of American cities. In Moscow, even the elite stores lacked the amenities and choice of a typical American supermarket.

He returned to Russia convinced of the bankruptcy of the communist system—and not just its financial bankruptcy but is moral bankruptcy. The United States was smaller than the Soviet Union; it had a smaller population and fewer natural resources. Yet, even poor Americans experienced a surplus that the average Russian would envy. An aide, Lev Sukhanov, stated that the incident caused Yeltsin to abandon Bolshevism.

Yeltsin became a voice against communism and quit the party in July 1990, just nine months after his visit to the Houston Randalls. By then, he had risen even higher in the Soviet political system and had been elected as the delegate from Sverdlosk to the Congress of People's Deputies of Russia with 72 percent of the vote. The next year, in July 1991, he ran in opposition to the Communist Party and was elected president of the Russian Federal Socialist Republic with 58 percent of the vote. Then, on September 18, 1991, communist hard-liners struck back. They launched a coup against Mikhail Gorbachev, who was then running the Soviet Union. Their plan was to roll back Gorbachev's free-market and elective-government reforms and restore traditional socialistic communism. The coup was foundered on three rocks: Gorbachev refused to resign, U.S. president George H.W. Bush refused to recognize the new Soviet government and Yeltsin refused to accept its legitimacy.

Yeltsin hurried to Moscow to resist the coup. When he got there, he climbed atop a Soviet tank in Red Square. From that perch, he gave an electrifying speech that defied the coup leaders and rallied the opposition. In the face of high-level intransigence and popular opposition, the coup collapsed, and Gorbachev was restored to power. This victory, however, did not matter. By the end of December 1991, the Soviet Union ceased to exist, member states withdrew and Yeltsin became the president of the independent Russian Federated Republic. Yeltsin remained in his position as president through the end of the decade and resigned in December 1999. During his time in power, he had mixed successes. He abolished socialism and replaced it with the capitalistic system that he had seen working well in Houston, he gave Russia a truly elective government and he fought off

The Randalls on the corner of Highway 3 and El Dorado moved to a bigger and better location back in the 1990s. It was shuttered afterward and stood empty for a decade. A smaller retailer, Food Town, rented the site and now operates at that location. *Photograph by author.*

a coup attempt. But he failed to rein in corruption and allowed himself to be replaced by Vladimir Putin. Like many leaders, he achieved great things despite his flaws, but he never delivered his full potential because of them.

As for the famous Randalls supermarket, it never surpassed that one moment of greatness. It was the latest and greatest thing in grocery stores when it first opened, but by the late 1980s, it was being superseded by larger supermarkets, even others that were within the Randalls chain. The grocery industry is ferociously competitive, and by the mid-1990s, the store was too small to meet the expectations of Randalls customers. It was shuttered shortly after the turn of the twenty-first century and stayed that way for several years. It was a forlorn sight in the boomtown of Houston. Yet, even old stores have second acts. That Randalls location was reopened as a Food Town around the twentieth anniversary of Yeltsin's visit. Food Town is a second-tier grocery chain, but at least the historic building is still in use—even if everyone has forgotten that it was a place that changed the world.

15.

THE RISE AND FALL
(AND RISE AND FALL AND RISE)
OF JIM WEST'S MANSION

So far, most of the stories in this book end with their subjects disappearing into obscurity. Occasionally, the subjects were repurposed, and their original significances largely forgotten, like the case of the Gragg Building and the Food Giant. At other times, the road to obscurity was detoured in a strange and unexpected way, and such is the case for the Jim West Mansion.

James Marion West Sr. was an early twentieth-century Texas businessman—a tycoon, if you will. Over the course of his life, he made a fortune in timber, ranching and oil, and in that order. Despite his later riches, West started life in a poor family. He was born in May 1871 to a family in Mississippi who could charitably be called subsistence farmers. In 1880, the family moved to Trinity County in East Texas. They settled on a farm and continued subsistence farming. The family's fortunes continued to decline, so West left school at age thirteen and started working as a water boy at the Trinity County Lumber Company. By the 1890s, he had worked his way up through the company and went into partnership with the mill's owner. Eventually, West bought out his old boss and started amassing his timber fortune. He later met and married Jesse Gertrude Dudley, a schoolteacher in Josserand, Texas. The couple had three children: James Jr., Westley and Mildred.

By 1910, West owned twenty-four lumber mills and was a millionaire several times over. West described himself as a cattleman at heart, and eventually branched off into that industry as well. In his late teens, West ran a few head of cattle on his family's land in Trinity County. West moved to Houston in 1905, where he invested heavily in cattle. Eventually, West became president of the Fort Terrett Ranch Company, a large spread that was about two hundred miles west of Austin. He later bought several spreads in Texas and New Mexico, and by the 1930s, his cattle herds numbered in the tens of thousands. His favorite ranch was the West Ranch near Houston, a thirty-thousand-acre range that covered most of the land that is now occupied by NASA, Clear Lake City and Southern Pasadena. The ranch reached as far west as the Galveston, Houston and Henderson Railroad, as far south as Clear Lake and as far east as Toddville Road.

After finding success in the ranching business, West went into the oil business in the 1920s, which was a good time for that business. He, along with his sons (who were adults by then), and Hugh Roy Cullen teamed up with one another and hit it big, making a third fortune. When oil was discovered on the West Ranch, he sold most of it to Humble Oil in exchange for cash and a chunk of Humble Oil stock.

Between West's death in 1941 and 1969, when the Lunar Science Institute (LSI) moved in, the West Mansion stood empty. Over the next twenty-two years, the LSI and its successor, the Lunar and Planetary Institute (LPI), made the West Mansion a place where science happened. *Courtesy of the Lunar and Planetary Institute.*

What do you do after you have made three fortunes? Well, West dabbled in politics—unusually for an early twentieth-century Texan—as a Republican. He also bought and ran newspapers in Austin and Dallas. In 1928, Jim and Jesse built a home, announcing that they had arrived as part of the Texas elite. The couple set their dream home on the West Ranch, just in view of Clear Lake (which was actually clear before the channel connecting Clear Lake to Galveston Bay was deepened). Joseph Finger, a noted Houston architect who went on to design the Jefferson Davis Hospital eight years later, designed the home. Finger had already racked up a slew of notable designs for buildings in Houston and Galveston by the time the Wests hired him.

The house took two years to design and build, and the result was a modest (measured against Versailles) forty-five-room, seventeen-thousand-square-foot Italian Renaissance villa that was located a mere one hundred feet from Clear Lake. The home had a nine-car garage, a formal garden, tennis courts, gazebos, barns and stables and a swimming pool with changing rooms. Since neither Jim nor Jesse intended to do any cooking or cleaning, the estate had outbuildings to house the estate's manager and staff. The exterior of the home was made of concrete and limestone and had tall casemate windows. The interior was composed of marble, tile, walnut and gold leaf. The house was lavishly decorated with silver sinks, Moorish wall tiles, Art Deco ceilings, Doric columns at the foot of the staircases and extensive decorative metalwork. There were nine bedrooms and nine bathrooms, along with a music room, a massive living room, a library, a den and a fifty-foot-long Palm Room that was used to host large parties. The entire estate cost $250,000 (around $3.75 million today).

The Wests moved into their new home in 1930 and remained there in splendor until Jim West Sr.'s death in 1941. Jesse moved out of the home and lived in Houston until her death in 1953. Although the mansion remained empty between 1941 and 1953, Jesse West kept the place maintained. After her death, Humble Oil purchased the house and the remainder of the West Ranch property and the maintenance of the house ceased. They lacked Jesse's sentimental attachment to the place and had no use for a forty-five-room residence that was twenty-five miles from downtown Houston, so the complex stood empty, unfurnished and unmaintained.

Meanwhile, a lot was happening around the neglected homestead. In 1961, Humble Oil gave NASA one thousand acres for the Johnson Space Center (JSC), and in the same year, it formed Friendswood Development Company. In 1963, Friendswood began building a master-planned community next to JSC and the West Mansion, which they called Clear Lake City. The West Mansion was kept as a reserve for the development, but it seemed that the building, which had been empty since 1941 and abandoned for over a decade, was down for the count. However, it made a phoenix-like recovery.

Johnson Space Center (the Manned Spaceflight center until August 1973) was the lead center for Project Apollo, the effort to put a man (NASA's Astronaut Corps would remain a boys' club until 1978, when the first women were accepted into the corps) on the moon and return him safely to Earth. The astronauts planned to return from the moon with souvenirs—moon rocks and lunar soil—so a lab was built at JSC to house the samples. The scientists that worked with these samples had to be housed somewhere. The space center was a boom town in the 1960s and, like most boom towns through history, was overcrowded. So, an offsite location that was within a convenient distance to the space center was sought for these new researchers.

Right next door to JSC was a thirty-five-thousand-square-foot location: the West Mansion. The home was a white elephant from the standpoint of Humble Oil; the company knew it would have to raze the property before it could develop it, which would have been expensive. In 1968, Humble Oil donated to Rice University the twenty-three-acre parcel containing the West Mansion, where the university housed the Lunar Science Institute (LSI), its new planetary sciences department. Later, the interests of the field expanded from the moon to the solar system, so in 1977, it was renamed the Lunar and Planetary Institute (LPI).

NASA gave a $580,000 grant (worth $4,400,000 today) to Rice University to renovate the building, which had stood abandoned for twenty-five years. This grant covered the cost of repairing the damage due to neglect and converting the outbuildings into offices. The Palm Room was even converted into a massive conference room. The LSI occupied its new home in 1969 and remained there for twenty-two years. It was an odd home; few research facilities come with marble floors, Moorish tile, massive chandeliers and elaborate decorative wood paneling. Mainframe computers, movable metal bookcases and (later) personal computers gave the place an anachronistic feel—an odd blending of the Space Age and the Gilded Age. Despite—or perhaps because of—its eccentricities, most of the personnel housed there loved the place.

For the first time, the mansion became well known. The area around Clear Lake was a largely rural area that Jim West Sr. used as a retreat, so he kept

After the LPI moved out, the mansion stood empty for another twenty years. By 2006, the place was looking run-down. *Photograph by author.*

it out of public view. If Houstonians thought about the place during West's occupancy of it, they thought of a private eccentricity of a very wealthy man. More typically, Houstonians focused on the public eccentricities of West's eldest son, James West Jr.; he was a boisterous extrovert who was better known to the public than his father. Houstonians called the younger James West "Silver Dollar" Jim West due to the younger man's habit of tossing handfuls of silver dollars into crowds of children.

As the home of the LSI, later the LPI, the building gained public attention for the first time. An annual Lunar and Planetary Science Conference was held annually in March; it started as the Apollo 11 Lunar Science Conference in 1970 before its name was changed in 1978. The first conferences were held at the West Mansion, which drew worldwide attention to the estate. JSC groups also held meetings in the West Mansion; some were business related, but others, such as the JSC Astronomical Society meetings, were reserved for off-hours activities and open to the public. The urbanization of the Clear Lake area also meant that a lot of people passed the mansion while commuting to work or heading out to enjoy a day on the water at Clear Lake. It had been called a landmark prior to its occupation by the LPI, but it had previously just been an invisible landmark. By the 1970s, it was part of the community.

By the late 1980s, the LPI had outgrown the West Mansion; the structure lacked the capabilities that were needed for a PC-intensive organization. The LPI received funding for a larger building—a conventional office building—and moved in 1991. At that time, the institute sold the West Mansion to Exxon, Humble Oil's successor, and the mansion was once again empty. Exxon had no use for the mansion but signed a deed restriction in 1992 that stated that the owner would "maintain and preserve the West Mansion and West Mansion land in good condition and not allow the West Mansion and West Mansion land to deteriorate or to demolish or allow the West Mansion to be demolished for a period of twenty years." In 1994, the mansion was sold to the Pappas family, who were restaurateurs. Perhaps they intended to put a restaurant in the house or refurbish it as a residence; whatever their original intention, they put it on the market in 2003. A preservation group attempted to purchase the property, but its efforts fell through.

In 2006, Hakeem Olajuwon, the longtime and all-star center for the Houston Rockets basketball team, bought the entire property, flipped it and sold it to Opus West, a development company that intended to convert the property into a senior living center. When Opus West went bankrupt in 2009, ownership of the property reverted to Olajuwon, but by then, the mansion was in rough shape. It had been unoccupied since 1992, and despite the deed restriction (which was set to expire in 2012), preventing deterioration had taken a low priority. Then, in 2013, everything changed. Olajuwon started a new line of high-end sports clothing called DR34M ("Dream" if

In 2013, Hakeem Olajuwon, who was—by then—the owner of the property, started DR34M, a men's fashion company. He chose the West Mansion as his corporate headquarters, and a major renovation followed. The place looks like a dream today. *Photograph by author.*

you squint at it right—Olajuwon's nickname during his basketball days was "Hakeem the Dream"), and he was in need of a headquarters and flagship store. He decided the West Mansion set the right tone for a place that sold $600 to $2,500 leather bags and $3,000 suits.

The mansion was completely renovated and sported fresh white paint and a red tile roof—by 2015, the old place was looking good. Even though it has not yet been opened to the public (its website states "NOT OPEN TO THE PUBLIC, MUST MAKE APPOINTMENT"), it is still being maintained in top condition. No one knows how the home's story will end. Maybe it will remain DR34M's headquarters as the company becomes the next big thing in fashion sportswear. Maybe Olajuwon will abandon the effort and the building will once again stand empty. As of 2020, Olajuwon will have occupied the mansion for seven years, which is not quite as long as the eleven years that Jim West Sr. was there but is still a respectable timespan. Even if Olajuwon dumps the place, the renovations he has done should keep it in reasonable shape for another two decades. That ought to be enough time to find a new use for the mansion—it always has been in the past.

BIBLIOGRAPHY

Bush, David. "West Mansion: Clear Lake." *Houston History Magazine* 5, no. 2. (Fall 2007): 19–22.

Day, James. *The Vanishing Vision: The Inside Story of Public Television.* Berkeley: University of California Press, 1995.

Fisher, James E. "KUHT-TV: The University of Houston's Second Great Vision." *Houston History Magazine* 10, no. 1. (Fall 2012): 30–34.

NASA. *Space News Roundup,* 1962–1972. Scanned archives of *Space News Roundup* from 1962–2001. www.historycollection.jsc.nasa.gov.

National Register of Historic Places Registration Form: James and Jessie West Mansion, Houston, Harris County. United States Department of the Interior, National Park Service, 1994.

Schroeder, Richard. *Texas Signs On: The Early Days of Radio and Television.* College Station: Texas A&M Press, 1998.

Sibley, Mary McAdams. *The Port of Houston: A History.* Austin: University of Texas Press, 1968.

Strom, Stephen R. *Houston Lost and Unbuilt.* Austin: University of Texas Press, 2010.

Texas State Historical Association. "The Handbook of Texas Online." Austin, TX. 2019. www.tshaonline.org.

Wasson, S. Deane. *Houston Cotton Exchange and Board of Trade Brochure: "Fifty Years a Cotton Market."* Houston, TX: Rein printing Company, 1924.

Woods, Herb. *Galveston–Houston Electric Railway.* Glendale, GA: Interurbans, 1959.

INDEX

W

Y

ABOUT THE AUTHOR

Mark Lardas, a sometime engineer, freelance writer, historian and model-maker, has lived in the Houston area for forty years. He is currently employed as a technical writer and spends his spare time collecting offbeat stories about Houston history. He worked on NASA's Space Shuttle program as a navigator and engineer from 1979 to 2011.

Printed in the USA
CPSIA information can be obtained
at www.ICGtesting.com
LVHW061630180923
756757LV00055B/377